PAUL THE PREACHER

RAYMOND BAILEY

BROADMAN PRESS
NASHVILLE, TENNESSEE

©Copyright 1991 ● Broadman Press
All rights reserved
4260-35
ISBN: 0-8054-6035-7
Dewey Decimal Classification: 225.92
Subject Heading: PAUL, APOSTLE
Library of Congress Card Catalog Number: 90-20084
Printed in the United States of America

Library of Congress Cataloging-in-Publication Data

Bailey, Raymond, 1938-
    Paul the preacher / Raymond Bailey.
        p. cm.
    Includes bibliographical references.
    ISBN: 0-8054-6035-7
    1. Paul, the Apostle, Saint. 2. Preaching--Biblical teaching.
I. Title.
BS2655.P8B35 1991
225.9'2--dc20
[B]
                                                                    90-20084
                                                                         CIP

This book is dedicated to
teachers driven by a passion for truth
who evoke in their students
a love for learning,
and who are used by God
to transform persons and society
through the renewal of minds (Rom. 12:2).

Contents

A Personal Word

As I wrote this book, especially Chapter 2, my thoughts turned to those persons and experiences that had shaped my life and ministry. This reflection infused the phrase *alma mater* with new meaning for me because the schools I have attended have truly been "nurturing mothers." My schools from elementary through post-graduate work have provided a climate of openness and challenge that evoked curiosity and new thought. The educational environments encouraged creative pursuit of truth, made learning a joy, and stimulated students to be "transformed by the renewal of your mind."

Schools are essentially faculties, collections of individuals who create the climate and give character to the institution. The most significant persons in my life have been schoolteachers. This is true of my spiritual as well as my mental development. I have been fortunate to have teachers who focused on values and thought processes rather than rote learning.

Paul was the product of the persons who had instilled in him knowledge and an intensity for life, life which was meaningful only when centered in God and God's wisdom which did not always conform to law and custom but was dynamic in a world still in process of becoming. Paul synthesized in himself a stream of influences from different sources and in this regard he is a model for all of us. My own sources had several things in common: they were creative; they were not afraid of truth; they loved teaching; and they were people of faith.

10

Paul the Preacher

My early years were influenced by teachers from first through twelfth grades who instilled a love for learning and a belief that learning could make a difference. Lois Boli, Miss Spruce, Ethel Masters, Helen Eckleman, and Virgil Mattingly were representative of the many who made learning a goal. Baylor University opened new vistas for me as I was exposed to liberal-arts education in a Christian environment. Bob Reid made history a living legacy shaping the future. Eddie Dwyer, Wally Christian, and James Wood demonstrated that theology was the queen of the sciences, that religion did not require you to be brain dead, and that God was the author of truth in every realm of human experience. It was Eddie Dwyer who first introduced me to a serious study of Pauline literature. (Mrs. Dwyer, by the way, was the college loan officer who pastorally kept me in school.) Paul Baker had tremendous influence on me as he taught me respect for the creative process and introduced me to intuitive ways of learning and creative ways of expression.

My love for rhetoric and the classics began with the study of Latin (in high school with Ethel Masters and in college with Roy Butler), but it was nurtured to a central concern for me by P. Merville Larson at Texas Tech University and Leland Griffin at Northwestern University. Lee Griffin taught me the basics of rhetorical criticism and demonstrated that rhetoric was not only an ancient art but a living instrument for good and evil.

The Southern Baptist Theological Seminary has been my family for over twenty years. I believe I received as good a theological education as is possible from the brilliant, dedicated people who taught me. As student, alumnus, and faculty member, I have been shaped by the great tradition of this Christian institution of higher learning. No institution could better blend the academic and practical aspects of ministerial training than Southern Seminary. The faculty is made up of scholar ministers committed to the search for truth, and to the service of the church and the world under the lordship of Jesus Christ.

The theology of Eric Rust, Glenn Hinson, Henlee Barnette, Frank Stagg, and many others is indelibly written across my mind.

11

A Personal Word

They have taught me to hear many ideas and then to arrive at my own conclusions, even when those conclusions were at variance with their own. Any small contribution I may make to theological education is due in large part to their influence.

The strength and integrity of the administration under the leadership of Roy Honeycutt encourages service to the denomination and the larger Christian community through writing. Dean Larry McSwain is sensitive to the needs of faculty and does all in his power to create a nurturing collegiality among the faculty. I am grateful to the Board of Trustees for a generous sabbatical policy that permits study leaves for contact with other scholars and settings that permit time to write. This book was written during a sabbatical leave.

Now a word about this book. It is a study written by a preacher, about preaching, for preachers. I hope others may find the content interesting and enlightening, but my rhetorical purpose is to improve the quality of preaching in the local church by introducing tested and proven biblical principles and skills.

I am grateful to Keitha Brasler for typing the manuscript, and to my colleagues, Dr. Craig Loscalzo and Dr. Estill Jones, for reading the original draft and making helpful comments.

Raymond Bailey

1

The Man Who Secularized the Gospel

Paul has occupied a place near Jesus in the center stage of Christendom from the beginnings of the movement. Adored by many as the faith's greatest hero, in recent history he has been assailed by some as a corrupter of the faith, and by others as the first Christian male chauvinist. Hardly anyone would deny that he was second only to Jesus in his influence on Christianity. He appeared on the scene when the church had no literature, no institutions, and only the beginnings of a community. He authored the first Christian literature and when the church sealed its canon, thirteen of the twenty-seven books of the New Testament were attributed to him. Students of Christianity may revere him or revile him, but none can ignore him.

All Things to All People

Paul was unquestionably the major interpreter of the implications of the incarnation and subsequent death and resurrection of Jesus the Christ, the promised deliverer of Israel and the unexpected hope of Gentile humanity. Paul was a person of great intelligence and with ideal educational and cultural preparation for the role he played in the development of Christianity as a world view, a faith system, an ethic for community, and an institution. Few persons possess the mental resources and broad empathies to be all things to all people in order that ". . . by all means" some might be saved, but Saul-Paul did. Christians find an easy explanation of the combination of incredible gifts and ideal experiences in the providence of God. Many believe that God ordained Paul for his mission while he was still in the womb. This viewpoint holds that

Paul the Preacher

God was preparing Paul to be the apostle on the Damascus Road. Saul-Paul, for whatever reasons, was the right person at the right time to further the ministry of the one born in the "fullness of time." Admirers and critics alike must recognize the extraordinary genius of the man called Paul.

It is unlikely that Paul would have become the great Christian missionary if his home had not been in this wider (Hellenistic) Judaism, if he had not been able to read and write Greek and possessed the Septuagint as his Bible, if he had not been used to accommodating himself to foreign customs, and if he had not had an eye for the wider world of highways by land and sea and for the great cities of the Mediterranean world.[1]

Add to this his Jewish heritage, his knowledge of the Hebrew scriptures, his religious enthusiasm, his training as a Pharisee, and you have a person who synthesized the best of East and West. His cross-cultural experience and education equipped him to free the message of God's revelation in Christ from Jewish moorings.

Paul's cosmopolitan outlook and liberal education, not to mention his adaptability to ethnic, cultural, and religious contexts, makes him subject to misinterpretation and vulnerable to criticism. He was in his own age, and has continued through the ages, to be a controversial figure. He has been identified with dualism, mainstream Judaism of his day, and corrupting Jewish Christianity with Greek philosophy. Nineteenth-century liberals accused him of creating a new religion unknown to Jesus: "Paul, it is alleged, turned Jesus' good tidings into a gospel of redemption replete with Jewish ideas and Hellenistic mythologies."[2] Paul synthesized many of these strands as the next stage of development of the Christian movement. Mainstream Christianity views him as one called of God through an extraordinary appearance of the risen Christ to extend the work of Christ in the power of the Spirit.

Interpretation and Application

Paul was not a teacher of Jesus' words but the interpreter of the meaning of the life, death, and resurrection of the Christ. He not only interpreted the revelation of Jesus for intellectual understanding but also for its implications about behavior. Paul applied the power of God's revelation in Christ to individual, family, community, and cosmic life. Individuals discover their source of life and their identity as children of God, heirs (Rom. 8:12-17). This newfound identity, the apostle taught, results in a different kind of community where gifts are shared and mutual respect and love prevail (Rom. 12:3-21). The new values affect the broader commonwealth of nations (Rom. 13:1-10). Christian freedom produces unthreatened people who have nothing to prove through pursuit of physical endurance and cultural success (Gal. 5:1—6:10). Paul advocated distinctively Christian family relations (Col. 3:18-25). Much of Paul's relational exhortation is pulled together in Ephesians 4:1—6:20 where words on relationship to the church, the world, in the family, and among social classes are pulled together. Paul's rhetoric was designed to transform the social order according to God's will by challenging individuals to allow (seek) personal transformation through the Spirit (Romans 8). Paul addressed people struggling with living in a world of choices, threats, and possibilities for families and political entities. He was not a philosopher concerned with theories, but a pastor-preacher concerned with living at all social levels and in the fullness of the life cycle. Theology for him was a practical matter.

Missionary, Theologian, Preacher

Paul demands our attention for three reasons: his role in the development of Christian faith and practice, as an instrument of truth, and as a model for ministry. Paul was the prototype Christian missionary. His strategies for expanding the power and influence of the good news remain viable and continue to be the focus of studies in missions and evangelism. Paul was an organizer and administrator. He trained leaders and delegated authority. He organized churches and established a pattern for cooperation among Christian communities in different locations and cultures. Paul appeared early in the drama of the church recorded in Acts and quickly became the central character. Luke portrayed Paul as the central figure and major hero of the liberation of the gospel from cultural bondage. While recognizing the special role of Israel in the plan of redemption, Paul understood that it was a role of responsibility rather than privilege and that God's intention was that through Israel all nations would be blessed; therefore, he proclaimed that Christ was good news for all people.

Paul was a theologian, the first writing theologian of the Christian era. He was a theologian in the purest sense: understanding God. He studied the revelation of God in historical and personal experience. He was not a self-conscious, systematic theologian in the sense that Augustine, Aquinas, or Calvin were, but he explored the meaning of God's revelation in Christ and the ramifications of that revelation for the cosmic and human orders. He was a student, teacher, and preacher of applied theology. Each of these facets of Paul's work is worthy of careful study but none is the focus of this work.

Paul was first and foremost a preacher of the gospel of Jesus Christ. In Acts Paul is idealized as the proclaimer of the gospel on the world stage. "Preaching was in fact, his calling, and with a fine single-mindedness he made it his life's work, everything else being subordinated to it."[3] Paul dominates the book of Acts as Jesus dominates the four Gospels. Scholars have disputed the historical accuracy of Acts, particularly with regard to the sermons but the church's canon, whatever the genre used, is what we have and is sufficient for our purpose. Acts, like other biblical literature, is itself preaching. Luke used historical methodology common to the ancient world, but for the rhetorical purpose of convincing readers of the truth of Christian faith. A. Q. Morton and James McLeman have argued that in Luke's Acts "we are in the presence of preaching in the form of history."[4] Dibelius wrote that one of the purposes of the writer of Acts was to instruct readers in the art of preaching.[5] He contends that Luke wanted to tell the story of the early church and to establish norms for the life of the church. The portrayal of Peter and Paul is intended to show what and how to preach. Through description of Paul's choice of occasions for

The Man Who Secularized the Gospel

preaching and of Paul's context, Luke created a paradigm for aspiring preachers. If the preaching of Paul in Acts is idealized, it is nonetheless a paradigm and the sermons attributed to Paul in that document will be a primary source for this study.

Words in Action

The Epistles will likewise be a source for our study of Paul the preacher, not only for his opinions on the subject but also as demonstrations of his practice. It is true that preaching is an oral art and that oral communication has a power lacking in written form. A great deal of work has been done on the oral traditions behind both Old and New Testament documents. The form critics aimed at the recovery of the oral history that lay behind the synoptic tradition. Walter J. Ong's study of *Orality and Literacy* should be read by every serious student of preaching. He reminds us that the oral character of our worship is no accident. God's power from creation was in His words. The Hebrews always thought of God as speaking and the biblical text itself exudes an oral mind-set. Ong notes that this oral character "even in its epistolary sections is overwhelming."[6] Exegetes struggle to get behind the script to the dynamic event, the social context that involved persons interacting.

> . . . in all the wonderful worlds that writing opens, the spoken word still resides and lives. Written texts all have to be related somehow, directly or indirectly, to the world of sound, the natural habitat of language, to yield their meanings. "Reading" a text means converting it to sound, aloud, or in the imagination . . . .[7]

Epistles, of all written materials, may come closest to oral communication. They tend to be dialogic in nature, either being written in response to previous expressions or inquiry or delivered in expectation of a reply. Paul wrote reluctantly. Time and again he told his readers that he would rather be with them, was planning to come to them soon, or could better explain to them in person.

Paul the Preacher

"Let such people understand that what we say by letter when absent, we do when present" (2 Cor. 10:11). He acknowledges the power of speech, which derives from Christ and is manifested . . . .[8]

We do well to remember that the Gospels were for years shared orally before given written form.

Paul's Corinthian correspondence is a nearly perfect example of written conversation. Scholars are generally agreed that First and Second Corinthians contain fragments of at least three letters presenting one side of an ongoing conversation. Paul's letters are far more lively than many public speeches.

. . . The style of his letters often changes from one section to another. The dialectic, both of the rabbinic method of inference and of popular philosophy with its smooth rhetoric, the conversational tone of personal discussion, the solemn style of his expression of thanks, the intense style of his confessions of faith . . . gives them their variety of colour . . . We can see that Paul dictated, so close is the written to the spoken word . . . .[9]

Only what was written in the pre-electronic ages could be preserved whether it was an oral debate accorded by a scribe, a sermon remembered and written, or a long-distance conversation in letter form.[10] There may be another reason for the distinctively oral character of Paul's epistles. Richard Ward has argued convincingly that they were written as performance literature; that is, Paul intended them to be read publicly in the churches and dictated them in a fashion conducive to that purpose.[11] One could reasonably contend that most, if not all, of the Bible is sermonic in nature. It is perhaps best understood as the preaching of the revelation of God. It may be said that unlike materials prepared for the eye such as novels or books and essays intended for silent comprehension, biblical documents are recordings (through the only means available at the time) of messages for the voice and ear. Such language is chosen and composed for its aural impact, which affects understanding and is a part of the message. Messages so framed require the participation of the hearers; they are designed to evoke a response.

19

The Man Who Secularized the Gospel

Reading powerful biblical passages can itself be preaching. The Bible conforms to that style of literature which Ong observes "has to be introduced uniquely into a unique situation, for in oral cultures an audience must be brought to respond, often vigorously."[12] Paul's writings fall into this category and instruct in the method of preaching as well as faith and practice. The frequent use of rhetorical questions by the apostle are one clue to his dialogic style. The exchange of letters indicated in Paul's letters confirm the conversational character of his preaching. Dialogue was a part of the Mars Hill event, and some of his most powerful statements are in the trial settings in Acts. The process and the content cannot be separated. The serious student of Pauline literature must ask not only what it means but also what it does.

There is ample evidence that Paul thought of himself primarily as a preacher. The power of God, he believed, was in the proclaimed word. His best known discourse on the subject is found in the tenth chapter of Romans where he eloquently declared that saving faith is a response to preaching. He indirectly described his own career as he wrote of those who are called and sent to propagate the message of Christ. Preaching was for Paul an "obligation" (Rom. 1:14). Preaching was a compulsion that could be denied only at great penalty (1 Cor. 9:16); it was the joy and purpose of his life. This book is a study of the preaching of Paul as a model for preachers of all generations.[13] This is not to say that contemporary preachers should preach in exactly the same way as Paul, but that they should approach preaching with the same attitude and philosophy as the great apostle. Paul did not sacralize form but allowed content to generate form and to transfuse existing forms and revitalize them.

Sanctified Rhetoric

Paul secularized the gospel by freeing it from the cultural bonds, religious and ethnic, of Judaism. It was not that he contaminated the gospel but rather that he infused the leaven of the gospel into the world. Paul translated the gospel into Western thought forms so that it could be apprehended by non-Jews. He adapted himself and his methods to various subcultures where he found opportunity to share his world view which was shaped by his experience with the Christ and the continuing presence of the Holy Spirit. Paul did not imitate the preaching of Jesus. His audience was different, the times were different, and even the message was different. Jesus spoke of the kingdom and of salvation but Paul preached the resurrected Christ as an event, a historical reality. Jesus the preacher became Jesus the preached in the ministry of the apostles.

The strategies employed by the evangelist were borrowed from the secular realm because he preached to secularists. Many of his hearers were unfamiliar with Jewish scriptures. His Hellenist background had apparently extensively exposed him to classical Greek rhetoric. Some people are offended at the suggestion that Paul used techniques popular in the pagan world. These critics interpret Paul's words in 1 Corinthians 1 and 2 as a repudiation of worldly philosophy and methodology. To many he appears to reject "debaters of this age" and their skills (1 Cor. 1:20*ff.*) A careful reading of that entire document as well as other epistles, however, discloses sections of classical polemic. First Corinthians itself is an excellent example of thoughtful Greco-Roman rhetoric, and all of Paul's epistles include examples. The diatribe, used extensively in Romans, has long been recognized by exegetes as a tool used by Paul. The diatribe was commonly used by Greek philosophers as a form of logical refutation. Paul's opening remarks to the Corinthians were self-deprecating, acknowledging his weakness and fears and assuring them that his message was not "in plausible words of wisdom" (1 Cor. 2:4). Such self-deprecation was (and is) itself a rhetorical device. This is not unlike Mark Antony of Shakespeare's "Julius Caesar" assuring the mob that he had not come to praise Caesar and then proceeding to do exactly that, or the public speaker who begins an address with "unaccustomed as I am to speaking in public." Paul did skillfully apply the art of classical rhetoric and modeled it well for application of its principles in modern pulpits.

The Man Who Secularized the Gospel

Perhaps the best defense of the use of classical rhetoric by Christians was written by Augustine in the fourth century.

> Who dare say that the defenders of truth should be unarmed against falsehood? While the proponents of error know the art of winning an audience to good will, attention, and open mind, shall the proponents of truth remain ignorant? While the sophist states facts concisely, clearly, plausibly, shall the preacher state them so that they are tedious to hear, hard to understand, hard to believe? While the one attacks truth and insinuates falsehood by fallacious argument, shall the other have too little skill either to defend the truth or to refute the false? Shall the one, stirring his hearers to error, urging them by the force of oratory, move them by terror, by pity, by joy, by encouragement, and the other slowly and coldly drowse for truth?[14]

George Kennedy contends that all religious movements are rhetorical by virtue of their intention to communicate truth.[15] He points out that the Bible is a rhetorical document in its intention to shape life. Paul's willingness to use all available means consistent with the message to transmit the truth gave to the church a great deal of freedom in methodology appropriate to the task. Unfortunately, the church has not always exercised the freedom and used all the resources available to proclaim the gospel.

Christian preaching as exemplified in Paul's work is distinguished from other forms of rhetoric only by content. Rhetoric is the use of reasoning, emotional appeal, and communication principles to achieve a particular purpose. An act is rhetorical when the agent intends to move the audience to new understanding or new behavior. The modern philosopher and critic Kenneth Burke identified the basic function of rhetoric as "the use of words by human agents to form attitudes or to induce actions in other human agents."[16] George Kennedy summarizes the province of rhetoric as "choice and arrangement of words" along with "the treatment of the subject matter, the use of evidence, the argumentation, and the control of emotion" to accomplish a speaker or writer's purpose.[17] Aristotle defined rhetoric simply as "discovering in the particular case what are the available means of persuasion."[18]

Paul did not shy away from the idea of persuasion in relationship to the gospel. Luke did not blush to report that Paul "argued in the synagogue every sabbath, and persuaded Jews and Greeks" (Acts 18:4) or that Demetrius recognized Paul's power as a debater who "persuaded and turned away a considerable company of people" (Acts 19:26). Paul believed he was accountable to God for his efforts to persuade people to respond to the grace of God (2 Cor. 5:11). He presented arguments so others might be "fully convinced" in their mind (Rom. 14:5). Not only did he set out to state his position clearly, he consciously sought to clear the way by rebutting the arguments of opponents. "We demolish arguments and every pretension that sets itself up against the knowledge of God" (2 Cor. 10:5, NIV). Paul was advocate and debater appealing for the minds of persons with all the tools available to him.

Elements of Rhetoric

By Paul's time, rhetoric was treated in five divisions: invention—subject matter; disposition—arrangement; elocution—style; pronunciation—delivery; and memory. Invention is the most important of the divisions. This division deals with the content of the speech. Paul was a seeker after truth, and when truth possessed him he was compelled to share it. The wisdom of the Greeks is indicated in their choice of invention to label this category. Preachers begin with the form of the truth as it has come to them and ask how it can be transmitted to others. The task may be understood as one of translation. Paul struggled to find a way to translate Hebrew tradition and experience so that it could be grasped by others. His experience with the Christ had to be related to the experience of others. The truth had to be made comprehensible and appealing.

Invention

Invention was subdivided into three modes of proof, *ethos, pathos,* and *logos. Ethos* is that power of proof that resides in the perceived credibility of the preacher. Do the hearers trust the

The Man Who Secularized the Gospel

speaker, and are they inclined to want to believe the message? *Pathos* refers to the emotional appeal of a message that promises to conform to the audience's values and goals. *Logos* has to do with the inherent logic in the message itself.

Aristotle taught that *ethos*, the perceived character of the speaker, "is the most potent of all the means of persuasion."[19] Who would deny the truth of his observation in the context of religious truth. Ultimate questions, knowledge, integrity and benevolence are personal qualities believed to produce credibility. Will the congregation believe that the speaker has authentic knowledge of the subject at hand? Is the preacher a trustworthy person who has the best interests of the audience at heart? Few contemporary Christians or neutral observers would question an abundance of these qualities in Paul, and yet Paul's authority was continually challenged. A great deal of his energy was expended defending his apostleship and teachings. Paul often struggled to distinguish himself from the traveling teachers, magicians, and preachers who manipulated the poor and uncritical people of the day. For purposes of persuasion it is not merely character that is important, but perception of character. The credibility of preachers does not depend on who they are but on who the audience thinks the preacher is. Reputation can be a positive or negative factor for the preacher. Remember, however, that Paul began his ministry under a cloud of suspicion. The Pharisees viewed him as a traitor, the Jews as a threat, and the Gentiles as an unknown.

Paul demonstrated his vast knowledge in the content of his messages as well as the credentials he was forced to present time and again. The epistles were written to Christians, but to those outside the church the position of apostle invoked no respect. Paul appealed to forms of authority appropriate to particular audiences. As an early missionary, Paul had only his experience, his skills, the Old Testament (without authority among most Gentiles) and the Holy Spirit. He gave evidence of knowledge of different schools of Hebrew law and different schools of Greek culture. He showed respect for cultural differences and demonstrated a knowledge of history. Paul was an effective teacher-preacher.

Integrity emerges from the being of the preacher. A preacher's credibility is rooted in what is perceived as personal spirituality and behavior. Paul wrote of mystical experiences and testified of visions (2 Cor. 12). Only a transcendent Christian experience could have kept him in the fray against such odds. He refused payment for his services so that he could not be accused of self-interest. He urged the Thessalonians to "abstain from every form of evil" (1 Thess. 5:22).

Benevolence, the audience's perception that the speaker genuinely has their best interests at heart, is the bridge that carries us into the second mode of proof, that of *pathos*. *Pathos* is the power of conviction that exists in the values, beliefs, and feelings already held by the audience. A wise speaker as well as a caring pastor takes measures to identify what is important to his or her audience; this includes what an audience wants and what they need. Paul refused to accept financial support and earned his own living in order to avoid accusations of ministry for profit (1 Cor. 9:1*ff.*; 2 Cor. 11:7-11; Acts 18:3). Benevolence was an element of his preaching as well as his practice; "let each of us please his neighbor for his good" (Rom. 15:2). Preachers who can demonstrate empathy with an audience, that is, convince them that they think like them, feel with them, suffer with them are assured of a sympathetic hearing.

Paul spent extended periods of time with people. He lived with them, worked with them, ate with them, used analogies from their common experience. Kenneth Burke cites identification as the key issue in persuasive communication. "You persuade a man," he writes, "only insofar as you can talk his language by speech, tonality, order, image, attitude, idea, *identifying* your ways with his."[20] Because he spent time with people, he knew what they felt and thought. He could appeal to their values. Aristotle wrote that advocates should study the emotions of their audiences to determine what favorably disposed them to act in a certain way. People act out of anger, love, fear, pity, hatred. Preachers should know what is likely to be the mental state of their hearers, who they care about, and what arouses their feelings.[21] Paul was a master of adaptation and identification. The message preached to Jews at Antioch in Pisidia (Acts 13:13*ff.*) was different in content and form from the one delivered to Greeks in Athens (Acts 17:16*ff.*).

Ethos and *pathos* are means to the end of transmitting the message which has a force of its own. The message of the apostles addressed the ultimate questions of life. They had to translate that message into a form appropriate to his importance. They set out to evangelize the world with only the Old Testament, personal experience with Christ, and the Holy Spirit. They had to invent a system of belief that would build a community. The emphasis here is on "system," showing the interrelatedness of the truth about God, humanity, and the ethics of Christian belief.

The preaching of Paul institutionalized a theology in order to preserve and promote it. He established the *stasis*, that is the issues to be debated and the images, figures of speech, and topics appropriate to discussion of Christianity. The Greeks and Romans developed a list of eight items to be included in argumentation. To be addressed are such questions as what is right, legal, advantageous, honorable, pleasant, easy, feasible, and necessary.[22] In one way or another these appear in Paul's discourses. Paul developed the central proposition of justification by faith and demonstrated its advantages to the law and faithlessness. He indicated that easy access had been provided by Christ, who had met the demands of the law and become righteousness for believers. Belief in Christ was proclaimed as necessary for appropriating God's grace.

Rhetoric was designed for use in matters not scientifically demonstrable. Orators took important matters that could not be empirically or rationally verified and offered an opinion about what was true. The speaker sought to lead the audience to an inferred conclusion based on the best evidence possible. Using the soundest logic possible, the speaker seeks to convince hearers that something is plausible, possible, probable. The goal is to establish the highest level of probability possible. In the case of the resurrection, one might begin with the possibility of a person rising from the dead, move to the likelihood or plausibility of Jesus having risen and hopefully convince listeners that the evidence (mostly testimony and the history of the church) infers that He did indeed rise. The rhetorician deals with that which is feasible but not measurable, demonstrable. Religious rhetoric falls into this category because God cannot be proved by laboratory methods. Scientific methods cannot "prove" "facts" of faith. George Kennedy points out that Christians developed a radical rhetoric based on a secret inner revelation, that is, an authority, power derived from direct illumination external to themselves. There is an obvious danger here because anyone can claim such revelation; it must, therefore, be tested against the testimony of others, Scriptures, personal intelligence, and experience.[23]

Arrangement

Invention is far and away the most important canon of rhetoric. Actions must be shown to be reasonable and advantageous. The remaining four elements are means to the end of communicating the message. Disposition has to do with the ordering of material in such a way as to conform to and stimulate natural thought processes. Arrangement is more important than some preachers suspect. Ordering has the purpose of leading the hearers in the process of thinking in such a way that they will arrive at the desired conclusion. A good sermon is not a collection of "points" but a sequential movement from one level of conviction to another. The well-crafted speech was expected to have four movements: introduction, statement of the case or proposition, arguments or evidence, and conclusion.

Purpose is the most important factor in determining the form of a message. Classical rhetoric recognized three types of speech: judicial, deliberative and epideictic. People form juries in places other than courts of law. Many evangelical groups governed by congregational polity require a candidate for a pastoral position to preach a "trial sermon." Sermons seek verdicts from uncommitted listeners. Judicial rhetoric focuses on past events and facts. Christian preachers ask people to judge the facticity of the resurrection.

A familiar proposition for Paul was that Jesus was the Messiah who was crucified and raised from the dead.

Deliberative persuasion addresses policy for the future. Burton Mack states that the majority of early Christian rhetoric was deliberative in that "every aspect of the new persuasion (including the imagination of founder figures and founding events, beliefs, behavior, and the adjudications of social issues) had to be approached as a matter of policy that would determine the future of . . . the community."[24] George Kennedy identifies the First Letter to the Thessalonians as deliberative because the purpose is to exhort the people to "stand fast in the Lord" (3:8) and to live holy lives (4:1-8).

Epideictic speeches are concerned with praise and blame and are set in the present. The issue is one of honor. Portions of various epistles fall clearly in this category as Paul praises co-workers. Much of Ephesians 1:3—3:21 is a reaffirmation of commonly held beliefs. The church is honored as a physical manifestation of the glory of God. Philippians 1:1—3:1 is characterized by praise of various persons and stresses the joy that results from the work of God in his people.

Style

Style has to do with the use of language, both its power to convey meaning and to evoke feeling. A picture is supposed to be worth a thousand words but one only has to read or listen to 1 Corinthians 13 or Philippians 2:5-11 to know that words have a beauty and power that often surpasses the visual. Classical writers conceived of language as symbolic action and the Hebrews had reverence for the power of words to create and destroy. Thought must be expressed in words. If the words are not right, the thoughts won't be.

Delivery

Delivery may be given too much or too little emphasis. Too many people get so focused on delivery, which is only the vehicle, that they neglect the content which is of supreme importance. The scriptural record seems to indicate that delivery was not Paul's strength; indeed, it was a weakness exploited by his adversaries: "For they say, 'His letters are weighty and strong, but his bodily presence is weak, and his speech of no account' " (2 Cor. 10:10). It should not be forgotten that many responded to his preaching and he was probably heard by more people than any of the other apostles. More will be said about this in Chapter 2.

Memory

Memory is not valued today as it was in ancient times. When every community did not have a library, radio, television, fax machine, or lap-top computer, the great teachers and leaders had to carry a great deal of information, evidence, and illustrative material in their heads. Paul's library was in the computer of his brain. Modern treatments of rhetoric rarely discuss the canon of memory because it seems antiquated, but Paul's memory was a powerful and important tool in his service.

Memory can be an important asset to the contemporary preacher. Memory may reflect a control of thought that frees the speaker from dependence on manuscripts and loss of rapport with the audience. Paul was ready to share his faith whenever the opportunity presented itself—in the marketplace, in prison, on board a ship, in the homes of friends, in formal or informal situations. Today's pastors are often given opportunity to express the Christian viewpoint in unexpected places and at odd times. The classical view of memory included a notion of information acquired, classified, and readily available. The preacher is expected to be a walking computer that can draw up biblical and theological knowledge at will. Moreover, clear images for translating that knowledge into relevant daily counsel must also be easily accessible.

Conclusion

Paul was one of the first preacher-missionary-evangelists but he also may have been the first self-conscious Christian rhetorician. Jewish philosophical and religious thought had to be explained in Gentile thought forms. New metaphors and analogies had to be invented to grasp the minds and imaginations of Greeks, some of whom had been introduced to Jewish people and culture and some of whom had not. Jewish Christians needed help understanding the implications of their faith for non-Jews and assistance in overcoming their prejudice toward those who had once, at least in their minds, been excluded from God's chosen. Jesus and Paul had good news for those who had been military and political enemies and commercial competitors with the Hebrews. Paul was the ideal person to bridge the cultural and religious chasm. He had a foot in both worlds and he, more than any other single individual, universalized the proclamation of God's in-breaking in human form in the world and God's offer of salvation to all who would receive it.

Paul secularized the gospel in the sense that he put it in forms that made it comprehensible to most of the known world of his day. Paul accomplished his task through the use of the most effective means of persuasion. He drew on the tried and proven methods of the classical rhetorical tradition as well as his personal willingness to be whatever the mission required. He models for the modern preacher effective homiletics for cross-cultural communication in a pluralistic society.

Notes

1. Martin Dibelius and Werner Georg Kummel, *Paul*, trans. Frank Clarke (Philadelphia: The Westminster Press, 1953), 21.

2. Gunther Bornkamm, *Paul*, trans. D. M. G. Stalker (New York: Harper and Row, 1971), 109.

3. Dibelius, 87.

4. A. Q. Morton and James McLeman, *Paul, the Man and the Myth: A Study in the Authorship of Greek Prose* (New York: Harper and Row, 1966), 109.

5. Dibelius, 11.

6. Walter J. Ong, *Orality and Literacy: The Technologizing of the Word* (New York: Methuen Press, 1982), 75.

7. Ibid., 8.

8. George A. Kennedy, *New Testament Interpretation Through Rhetorical Criticism* (Chapel Hill: University of North Carolina Press, 1984), 94.

9. Dibelius, 99.

10. A concise and stimulating discussion of the special character of New Testament documents can be found in Amos Wilder, *Early Christian Rhetoric: The*

30

Paul the Preacher

Language of the Gospel (Cambridge: Harvard University Press, 1971); cf. Amos Wilder, *The New Voice: Religion, Literature, Hermeneutics* (New York: Herder and Herder, 1969).

11. Richard Finley Ward, "Paul and the Politics of Performance at Corinth: A Study of 2 Corinthians 10-13," (Ph.D. diss., Northwestern University, 1987).

12. Ong, 42.

13. The preaching of Paul has been examined from a number of different perspectives. John William Beaudean, Jr's, work *Paul's Theology of Preaching* (Macon, Georgia: Mercer University Press, 1988) includes an excellent bibliography on the subject as well as analysis of selected biblical passages from unchallenged Pauline works. See especially Jerome Murphy-O'Conner, *Paul on Preaching* (New York: Sheed and Ward, 1963) and Daniel Patte's *Preaching Paul* (Philadelphia: Fortress Press, 1984), surprisingly omitted from Beaudean's work.

14. Quoted by Charles S. Baldwin, "St. Augustine on Preaching," *The Province of Rhetoric*, ed. Joseph Schwartz and John A. Rycenga (New York: The Ronald Press Co., 1965), 162.

15. Kennedy, 158.

16. Kenneth Burke, *A Rhetoric of Motives* (New York: Prentice Hall, 1950), 41. Craig Loscalzo has explored the implications of Burke's work for preaching in "The Rhetoric of Kenneth Burke as a Methodology for Preaching," (Ph.D. diss., The Southern Baptist Theological Seminary, 1988).

17. Kennedy, 3.

18. Aristotle, *The Rhetoric of Aristotle* (Englewood Cliffs, N.J.: Prentice-Hall, 1960), 7. All subsequent citations refer to this edition.

19. Ibid., 9.

20. Burke, 55. His italics.

21. Aristotle, 92*ff.*

22. Burton L. Mack, *Rhetoric and the New Testament* (Minneapolis: Fortress Press, 1990), 37*ff.*

23. Kennedy, 54-96.

24. Ibid., 35.

2

God's Ulysses

I am a part of all that I have met;
Yet all experience is an arch wherethro'
Gleams that untravell'd world whose margin fades
For ever and for ever when I move.
How dull it is to pause, to make an end,
To rust unburnish'd, not to shine in use!
As tho' to breathe were life! Life piled on life
Were all too little, and of one to me
Little remains; but every hour is saved
From that eternal silence, something more,
A bringer of new things; and vile it were
For some three suns to store and hoard myself,
And this gray spirit yearning in desire
To follow knowledge like a sinking star,
Beyond the utmost bound of human thought.

These lines from Tennyson's "Ulysses" describe Paul—the man and the mission. Paul had a breadth of experience rare for his age. He was one of those gifted persons who synthesized the best of diverse cultures and philosophies. He was a part of all he had met and "a bringer of new things," one who followed "knowledge . . . beyond the utmost of human thought." He was led by God into the ultimate questions and some of the ultimate answers. God brought out of the traditions combined in Paul a totally new thing, the Christian church.

There is actually more biblical data about Paul's biography and formation than there is about Jesus. The autobiographical passages in Paul's writings are supplemented by the material in the book of Acts. Paul is the central character in the unfolding drama of the early church recorded by Luke. Many scholars discount Luke as a historical source because the book does not follow today's standards for historiography. However, Luke's methods were consistent with historians of that age. He wrote salvation history, and Paul's biography was incidental to his purpose of describing "the development and growth of the early Church from its origins in Jerusalem to its expansion as far as Rome"[1] and, I might add, to show how that development was under the power of the Holy Spirit. Luke's personal knowledge of the apostle was enriched by the fresh memories of others but demonstrates no acquaintance with Paul's epistles. Luke nowhere cites material from the epistles that bear Paul's name.

The person and proclamation of this early preacher are inextricably bound together. Paul's writings reflected his experiences and are a mixture of testimony and interpretation of God's revelation through human experience. He applied certain teachings of Jesus and of the Old Testament to situations in the churches he served.

Cosmopolitan from the Start

Paul was born in Tarsus, "no ordinary city" (Acts 21:39; 22:3). The city was a busy riverport located three miles from the sea. The city was a center of learning which the scholar Strabo declared surpassed Athens and Alexandria. Tarsus was a pluralistic, metropolitan area with representatives of the popular religions. Citizens were exposed to the arts and good literature. Paul's family enjoyed special status for Jews—they were Roman citizens—a fact that served Paul's ministry well (Acts 16:37; 22:28).

Paul's family prepared him in a number of ways to live in two worlds, one Jewish and the other Greco-Roman. Identification with the Romans was made easier by familiarity with their language and customs and even a Roman name. Some have speculated that Saul became "Paul" as a result of his conversion and mission, but it was not uncommon for families like Paul's to give their children a Jewish and a Roman name. All of his life he was both Saul and Paul. Luke's account of Paul's conversion makes no mention of a change of names (Acts 9). The name shift in the

Scriptures occurs at the beginning of the mission to the Gentiles where it is simply noted that Saul was also called Paul (Acts 13:9). The two names gave Paul identity in whichever world he found himself at a given moment.

Evidence of the early influence of his Greek environment is also found in the fact that Paul's Old Testament quotations are from the Septuagint which was the oldest Greek version of the Hebrew Scriptures. This translation had been completed by the end of the second century before Christ. It employs Greek idioms as well as Greek words and Paul's familiarity with it undoubtedly facilitated his interpretation of such important Jewish ideas as sin, righteousness, messianic hope, and the Kingdom for non-Hebrews. He could think in Hebrew imagery or the more conceptual Greek thought patterns.

The importance of Paul's living in a family with openness to other cultures and movement among diverse peoples as well as his being bilingual from childhood is obvious. Paul was never provincial in outlook and experience. He was not reared in a Jewish ghetto. From childhood he was aware of many religions and philosophies and had to deal with intellectual conflict. Christians today are often reared in ghettos more restrictive in experience and thought than Paul's. Americans are less likely to study other languages than citizens of other nations. Christians often develop a special language of Zion that is foreign to non-believers. In spite of the spread of cults and Eastern religions in the United States, few ministers trouble themselves to study comparative religion or even the art and culture of other nations. Some neglect even the study of ethnic subcultures in cities where they live and preach. The failure of Christians to learn the language, beliefs, and customs of others prevents believers from being as effective in sharing their faith as they could be. Paul devoured the knowledge available to him through formal education and everyday experience. Paul brought all of his human experience into submission to serve the evangelical task.

There were very practical aspects of Paul's early environment that likely exercised a positive influence on his ministry. I have already noted that he was used to being with people different from him. He was comfortable with people whose skins were different hues and whose eyes and noses were not exactly like his. There is a great difference in being reared in a village and in a metropolitan area. He was familiar with more complicated city life. Corinth, Ephesus, even Rome were no threat to a citizen of Tarsus. He knew about commercialism, hucksters, thieves, and street people, as well as academics, artists, and craftspersons. Traffic and crowds never threatened him. At a time when many people never wandered more than a few miles from home, when there was no radio or television, Paul traveled extensively as a youth. He was sent to Jerusalem to study "at the feet of Gamaliel" and be "educated according to the strict manner of the law of our fathers" (Acts 22:3). The world of Saul-Paul was larger than that of most of his contemporaries. His intellectual, cultural, and physical world dwarfed that of the average person of his day.

Stoic?

Paul's thought and language show evidence of a particular school of philosophy to which he was undoubtedly exposed in Tarsus. Stoicism was popular and prestigious. The strong ethic of the Stoics appealed to all social classes. Itinerant preachers did not originate with Judaism or Christianity. James Stewart wrote that Stoic evangelists (whom he compared to Salvation Army missioners) could be found wherever there were crowds of people in Asia Minor and Europe.

> The deep things of the soul, the answer to the universal quest for happiness, the need for moral reformation and spiritual rebirth, the way to victory over life and death—these were the themes on which the Stoic orator discussed with all the eloquence and appeal at his command.[2]

Paul found in Christianity values common to Stoicism: responsible freedom, duty, and virtue. He came to believe, however, that these qualities emerged from the divine creator and could only be sustained by the power of the Spirit. The standards were not human in origin but rather emerged from and were to be judged by the righteousness of God. The standards were transcendent and would be fully realized only in the eschaton. Perhaps of greater importance for this study was the apparent influence of the style of itinerant Stoic preachers.

> Salient features of the style of the Diatribes, as the Stoic discourses were called, were their rhetorical questions, their preference for short disconnected sentences, their use of the device of an imaginary objector, their flinging backwards and forwards of challenge and rejoinder their concrete illustrations from life.[3]

These are characteristics of good oral style and are prominent in Paul's recorded communication. Paul's use of parallels to Greek literature and his obvious respect for the natural order suggest a strong influence.

Paul was greatly influenced by his Greek environment but he was a Jew in temperament and training; "circumcised on the eighth day, of the people of Israel, of the tribe of Benjamin, a Hebrew born of Hebrews; as to the law a Pharisee . . . ." (Phil. 3:5). As noted above, Luke records that Paul was sent to Jerusalem for education in the school of Gamaliel. Gamaliel's school represented the liberal wing of Pharisaism. Acts portrays him as a tolerant leader who urged the Jews to exercise moderation toward the Christians. He did not seem to fear new ideas as his pupil did (Acts 5:34-39).

Pharisee

Those familiar with the Christian ministry of Paul should not be surprised that the apostle was a Pharisee. He was an intense man and a serious student. Paul brought his enormous intellect and great energy to bear on whatever task he undertook. The Pharisees have not been given fair treatment by most Christians. Their excesses are magnified in the New Testament because of their resistance and opposition to Jesus and their persecution of Paul. The Pharisees played an important role in preserving tradition and making practical application of faith to everyday life at a critical time in the life of the nation.

Pharisees are not mentioned in the Old Testament. They emerged during the two centuries preceding the Christian era. The word means "separated" and the movement's origin is traced to the Hasidim, the pious Jews who resisted the desecration of the temple and general religious persecution that climaxed under Antiochus IV. The Pharisees were middle-class laymen who stood firmly opposed to Hellenization among their fellow Hebrews. They were intolerant of Hebrews who cooperated with the occupation forces and adopted Western life-styles. The Pharisees stressed the implications of their faith for everyday living. As is often the case with defenders of the faith they were overzealous and their extreme legalism earned them the severe criticism attributed to Jesus throughout the New Testament and reaching a crescendo in Matthew 23:1-36 (cf. Mark 12:38-40; Luke 20:45-47).

Contemporary readers should not allow the faults of the Pharisees to blind them to their positive qualities. The Pharisees were committed to faithfulness to the law as they understood it. Their concept of law was broader than that of other groups of their day. Law was not limited in their minds to legal codes but embraced the will of God as expressed in the Torah and the Writings and the Prophets. The Pentateuch was certainly the heart of their system but there was knowledge of and respect for all the Scriptures available to them. They developed an oral tradition of interpretation of the Scriptures to apply to nearly every conceivable life situation. The Pharisees believed in a system of rewards and punishments based on obedience to the law. Obedience to the law purified the Jewish people for the future life to come through bodily resurrection. Paul's position on the law is often misrepresented. Paul did not reject the law except as a means of salvation. The law had been for Israel and for him a teacher, a revealer that established the need for salvation.

Paul's intense training in the Scripture, instruction in exegesis, sense of the practicality of the law, hope for the resurrection, and respect for morality were a part of his Pharisaical heritage that prepared him for the greater revelation of God in Jesus Christ. "When the Diaspora Jew Paul chose to become a Pharisee, he also decided to be a Jewish missionary to the Gentiles along the lines taken by orthodoxy, and was actually such before becoming a Christian."[4] His preaching, in content and form, was shaped by his Jewish and Hellenistic background. This was true in terms of what he accepted and what he rejected. He knew that the law could not produce salvation and he knew that the righteousness of God was the norm for all of life.

Exegete

Paul's use of the Old Testament indicates that he learned exegesis from the rabbinic schools. Paul's selection of passages and pattern of stacking them in support of a position was characteristic of rabbinic style. He learned the still-popular art of proof-texting from the Pharisees. Stewart cites Romans 9—11 as a striking example of this technique.[5] Text after text is cited in support of the privileged position of Israel among the peoples of the world. Paul showed no signs of feeling bound to the context of a passage.

> Thus in Deuteronomy 30:12*ff.* the great passage beginning "It is not in heaven, that thou shouldest say, Who shall go up for us to heaven, and bring it unto us?" asserted the claims and the practicability of the law: but when it appears in Romans 10:6*ff.* (KJV), what it asserts is the exact reverse—that faith, not law is man's salvation.[6]

Paul put what the canon infers are inspired thoughts into a free use of the text. It is true that a text, particularly an inspired text, takes on a life of its own and may have a meaning that was not in the mind of the original speaker or writer. Paul's exegetical practice is fraught with dangers for the modern interpreter who cannot claim the special degree of inspiration Paul possessed. Without Paul's direct inspiration the modern preacher should exercise far more caution in exegesis.

Paul demonstrated that he treated language and narration as mere vehicles of truth and not as sacred relics. Paul's experience compelled him to see God's truth as unfolding. Paul did not just interpret Scripture literally; he treated it as figurative in many instances. The allegorical mode of interpretation occasionally employed by the preacher was drawn from the hermeneutics of the rabbis. Christian allegory reached its zenith in the work of Origen and then faded as an acceptable method. Allegorists assume that biblical passages have several layers of meaning and that the simplest passage may have a deep hidden meaning which only the inspired exegete can discover. The clearest example of Pauline allegory is found in Galatians 4:21-31 where Paul states that the Old Testament story of Hagar and Sarah is an allegory which he proceeds to interpret. Each woman is depicted as a representative of a covenant, one of slavery, the other of freedom. Another example is found in 1 Corinthians 10:1*ff.,* where the Apostle describes the crossing of the sea as baptism and the rock that produced saving water in the desert as Christ: "For they drank from the supernatural Rock which followed them, and the Rock was Christ" (10:4).

Leather-worker

We know little about Saul-Paul from his youth until shortly before his conversion. We know that he learned the trade of tentmaking (Acts 18:3) or Dibelius suggests the more general "leather-worker."[7] As noted above Pharisees were laity and earned nothing from their religious service. Even the rabbis had to have other sources of income. Paul represented the tradition well in his pride in financial independence. While defending the right of ministers to be paid for their services, he boasted that he had accepted no remuneration for his labors (1 Cor. 9:1-18).

Family Man?

Paul's marital status is a matter of speculation. David Smith upholds the traditional view that for Jews marriage was a sacred obligation.[8] He contends that as a strict Pharisee and devout Jew, Paul was surely married and a widower by the time he appeared on the stage of the New Testament. Paul wrote of his singleness (1 Cor. 7:8) but did not make clear whether or not he had ever been

God's Ulysses

in another marital state. Dibelius on the other hand insists that Paul was never married.[9] It is certain that he was not married at the time of his mission work and thus enjoyed a remarkable freedom to go anywhere and say anything without fear of the consequences for family. Even Paul's singleness contributed to his ability to carry out the mission to the Gentiles. He did not have to worry about the possible effects his death might have on a family or whether or not a wife and children had the necessities of life while he sat in prison.[10] One's ministry is always affected by family concerns and status.

Christian

Paul's life and service as a Christian is well documented. It is remarkable that so devout a Pharisee as Paul, consumed with a desire to keep his religion pure, never encountered Jesus during his ministry. Perhaps Paul did not want to dignify the teaching of the untutored Nazarene by going to hear Him. The reports of Jesus' heresies may have been sufficient to evoke the intense hostility that motivated Saul's persecution of the embryonic movement. His devotion to the law aroused animosity toward those challenging Jewish orthodoxy and the hallowed traditions of his people. Bornkamm points out that it was not Jesus' messianic claims alone that provoked Saul's zeal as persecutor because there were frequently messianic pretenders on the Palestinian scene. Paul was motivated by the Christian attacks on the law and by his own evangelistic fervor for the orthodoxy of the Pharisees.[11] The popularity of the new movement and its appeal to devout Jews was more than the Pharisees could tolerate. Paul was determined to silence what he considered a dangerous heresy. He waged a holy war because he was "a Hebrew of Hebrews; as to the law a Pharisee, as to zeal a persecutor of the church, as to righteousness under the law blameless" (Phil. 3:5-6; cf. 1 Cor. 15:9). He was a cheerleader at the stoning of Stephen, encouraging acts of violence believing that the end justified the means (Acts 26:10-11). He indicated that he initiated the spread of the persecution (Acts 26:11-12).

Paul the Preacher

Called to Preach

It was on a mission of persecution that Paul was apprehended by the One he persecuted. His zeal would not be destroyed, only refocused. Most familiar to Christians is the dramatic account of Paul's encounter with Christ recorded in Acts 9. There was the great light, the appearance of the Lord, blindness, and the explanation of Ananias. Paul never recounts these events in the epistles. More important to him than the bizarre confrontation was the revelation of truth. He identified what was significant to him in the concise Galatian reflection: "He who had set me apart before I was born, and had called me through his grace, was pleased to reveal his Son to me . . . ." (1:15-16). It is interesting that the bizarre experience that fascinates so many modern preachers was not a major emphasis in the writings of the apostle. Paul focused on the message rather than the personal experience. The result of the revelation of the Son was a totally transformed view of life.

> But whatever gain I had, I counted as loss for the sake of Christ. Indeed I count everything as loss because of the surpassing worth of knowing Christ Jesus my Lord. For his sake I have suffered the loss of all things . . . that I may gain Christ and be found in him, not having a righteousness of my own based on law, but that which is through faith in Christ, the righteousness from God that depends on faith; that I may know him and the power of his resurrection. . . . (Phil. 3:7-11).

Paul's graphic descriptions of humanity's base nature and resulting immorality leads readers to think of conversion only in terms of turning from unspeakable wickedness to clean living. Dibelius makes an important observation leading to a different conclusion:

> Paul was not "converted" from a life of sin to a life of righteousness; one might rather say that he turned from a religion of righteousness to a religion of the sinner. Nor was he "converted" from a false god to the one true God, but from a wrong way of honouring God to the right way . . . .[12]

His was not a case of faithlessness finding faith but of misguided faith being redirected. This is important in understanding theology as opposed to moralism. Paul was already a moral man in his practice and a moralist in his teaching. In the first century as in the twentieth there were non-believers with high moral standards and other religions with moral imperatives stricter than Christianity, with a longer list of do's and don't's. The proclamation of Paul will not allow one to reduce Christianity to moralism.

Paul, because of his own experience, understood that there is religion that makes people sick and religion that makes people well. The sick religion of legalism gave false assurance and bound adherents while the good news of Jesus Christ set people free. The apostle preached freedom for the mind as well as the senses. He understood sin as a matter of relationship with God, a state of being that produced certain kinds of unhealthy behavior and failed to produce wholesome living. "For freedom Christ has set us free," he wrote the Galatian Christians, "stand fast therefore, and do not submit again to a yoke of slavery" (5:1). A disciple of Paul's school of homiletics will preach good news of liberation. Every Christian sermon should have some good news in it. The preachers should emphasize the "yes" of God to estranged humanity. "For the Son of God, Jesus Christ, whom we preached among you, Silvanus and Timothy and I was not Yes and No; but in him it is always Yes" (2 Cor. 1:19).

A significant aspect of Paul's sense of what happened on the Damascus Road was a clear call to preach. His encounter with Christ set him apart and called him "in order that I might preach him among the Gentiles" (Gal. 1:15-16). His call was comparable in form and ramifications to the calls of the great prophets (Jer. 1:5; Isa. 49:1; 6:8-9; Ezek. 1:1-2). His life was dominated by the inward compulsion to preach. He was called to preach a particular message to a particular people. The call was confirmed in a trance as the door opened for his work (Acts 22:21). Like the prophet of old there was a fire in his bones (Jer. 20:9); "necessity is laid upon me. Woe to me if I do not preach the gospel!" (1 Cor. 9:16). A distinct sense of a divine call impels the proclaimer to the difficult task of mental and spiritual preparation, the tough task of confronting persons with the gospel, the physical and psychological pressures that go with the vocation. Paul found in his call the force sufficient to the direction of his life. Old friends and former colleagues became enemies, and new friends came slowly because of suspicion based on his former ways. Only a strong sense that he was being obedient to a divine mandate could have sustained him through the beatings, imprisonments, persecution, and close escapes from death.

The Desert

Galatians also provides us with a personal chronology of the new convert's activities. It gives us some knowledge of a lengthy period about which Acts is silent. According to his own testimony, Paul "went away into Arabia." Paul's fellow Pharisees were stung by his apparent defection, and it is no surprise that they turned their wrath on him. Christians on the other hand greeted this sudden change with suspicion and were not about to welcome him into their circle and make themselves vulnerable to his persecution. Threats from both sides forced his quick nocturnal departure from Damascus (2 Cor. 11:32; Acts 9:24-25). We know little about the next ten years of the apostle's life. Some have speculated that this was a period of desert preparation filled with meditation on the Scriptures and spiritual communion. It is likely that it was there that his mysticism developed. He wrote to the Corinthians in his Second Epistle of "a man in Christ who fourteen years ago was caught up to the third heaven" (12:2) and of an "abundance of revelations" (12:7). The desert may well have been the environment that invoked his in-Christ mysticism (Gal. 2:20). It may have been during this formative period that Paul developed his strong sense of the mystical in-dwelling of Christ in himself and in all believers (Gal. 4:19; 2 Cor. 13:5; Rom. 8:10; Phil. 1:20; 2 Cor. 13:3).[13] He was not, however, a monkish recluse in this interval. During this period he made his first post-conversion trip to Jerusalem where he spent two weeks with Peter before returning to do missionary work in Syria and Cilicia (Gal. 1:18-21) where he built

God's Ulysses

a reputation as a preacher. His fame reached the mainline churches where it was reported that "he who once persecuted us is now preaching the faith he once tried to destroy" (Gal. 1:23; cf. Acts 15:23,36,41).

Those called to preach in any era would do well to take into account this period of seasoning. The flow of the Acts narrative leaves the reader with the impression that Paul immediately became the great preacher-theologian. This was not the case. As brilliant as he was, as well schooled as he was, and with a dramatic experience of the presence of Christ, Paul required an extensive period of preparation. It is tragic that many young men and women who experience God's call to service are impatient and unwilling to equip themselves for ministry. Without Paul's cultural experience, travel, linguistic skill, knowledge of the Scriptures, general education, and public experience, they want to plunge into ministry. The work of Christ is often damaged by zealous but untrained ministers.

Antioch Versus Jerusalem

Paul's success in his apprenticeship did not go unnoticed by Barnabas, a leader in the church at Antioch, who brought Paul to the place where his most productive period would be launched (Acts 11:26). Barnabas had much in common with Paul. Born in Cyprus, he too had a foot in each world. He had interceded for Paul with the first apostles (Acts 9:27) and was leading the work in Antioch where the church seems to have been more inclusive evangelizing Gentiles (Acts 11:20).

While Paul was in Antioch one of the most important events in the early history of the church occurred. Paul recalled the event in his letter to the Galatians in the context of his vigorous attack on legalism. Luke places the account of the Jerusalem Council at the center of his history (Acts 15). The immediate issue was circumcision, which was to the Jews the sign and seal of the covenant. The greater issue was the entire legal system as the means of becoming righteous. Paul returned to Jerusalem for the first time in fourteen years. It had been seventeen years since his conversion, and he had paid his dues; he had earned the right to be heard by "James, Cephas and John, who were reputed to be pillars" of the church (Gal. 2:9). The results of this council set the course for the mission of the church. The council rejected the possible subjection of Christianity to Judaism. It further allowed for diversity in theology and practice in the church. Total unity was not achieved. Issues of social relationship between Jews and Gentiles remained unresolved, but each had accepted the right of the other to exist as a part of the Christian community. The factions departed with mutual agreement on the obligations of Christian charity; "they would have us remember the poor, which very thing I was eager to do" (Gal. 2:10).[14]

The most important thing about the conference is what it revealed about Paul as a man with confidence in his theology and courage to defend it in the highest councils. He had clearly become the leader of the church at Antioch and of the emerging Gentile mission. The results of the conference suggest that he had harnessed his considerable gift in persuasion for the service of God. He was able to engage the most respected teachers and preachers in dialogue and convince them of the viability of his position. Paul demonstrated that his thoughts were ordered and that he was effective as a speaker.

Much has been made of Paul's report of his adversaries' assessment of his physical presence. According to him, "they say, 'His letters are weighty and strong, but his bodily presence is weak, and his speech of no account' " (2 Cor. 10:10). We should remember, however, that he was reporting the opinion of those who were seeking to discredit him. It is also worth noting that this was a situation in which he was being compared to "superlative apostles" (2 Cor. 11:5; 12:11) who were exceptional orators. One of them was Apollos who is portrayed in Acts as "eloquent" and "fervent in spirit" (Acts 18:24-26). Paul's success at Jerusalem indicates that he was effective if not eloquent. The churches he founded resulted from his presence and speaking. Problems arose when he was absent, and it was the absence that necessitated the written correspondence. He thought that he could win the minds of those questioning his views if he could speak to them face to face; therefore, he wrote of his desire to be among them and urged them to hold on until he got there to straighten them out. He wrote to his performance reviewers at Corinth that "I am not in the least inferior to these superlative apostles" and "even if I am unskilled in speaking, I am not in knowledge" (2 Cor. 11:5-6). Note the "even" and remember that Paul most often communicated his knowledge in person. Paul's way of dealing with the critical problems in the Jerusalem Council and his success say much about his intentional rhetoric and his rhetorical skill.

The Strength of Weakness

Paul's ministry was certainly affected by his weakness. His faithfulness did not deliver him from pain and disappointment. Paul boasted that he served out of weakness rather than strength (2 Cor. 12:5). He suffered from some chronic illness that was a "thorn in the flesh" (2 Cor. 12:7). Three times he prayed for healing but became convinced that God did not intend to heal him. His weakness was a constant reminder that it was God's strength upon which he had to rely. Krister Stendahl suggests that Paul was referring to his health problem in 1 Corinthians 2:3 and 1 Thessalonians 2:18. Stendahl thinks that the "hindrance of Satan" that prevented his traveling to Thessalonica was the illness blamed on Satan in 2 Corinthians 12.[15] Paul referred again to a "bodily ailment" in Galatians 4:13. Paul knew what it was to hurt and he knew what it was to have prayer requests unanswered or refused.

Passion and Patience

Paul's passion to carry the gospel as quickly as possible to the Gentile world was fueled by two compelling convictions. First, he was convinced that the experience on the road to Damascus was a clear call to preach Christ to the Gentiles (Gal. 1:16; cf. Rom. 1:14, 15:15-16; 1 Cor. 9:16). Christ had reconciled Paul to Himself and assigned him the role of minister of reconciliation between Jew and Gentile, God and humanity (2 Cor. 5:18,20). Secondly, the apostles anticipated the quick return of the Lord (1 Thess

5:1*ff*.; 2 Thess. 2:1*ff*.) When Paul began his ministry he expected to see the return of the Lord before his death. He sought to give Christians an ethic by which they could live happily and bear witness to the Christ "until he comes" (1 Cor. 11:26). This latter conviction gave to Paul's preaching a sense of urgency that is often lacking in contemporary proclamation. A preacher who lives with the expectation that this may be the year, the month, the week, even the day when history is consummated in Christ will have passion that others lack.

Paul's fervor and confidence in his call and message was subject to misinterpretation as arrogance. Paul by manner and message demanded a response to Christ which was difficult to separate from a response to Paul. Humans find it almost impossible to separate the message from the messenger. This is again the scandal of particularity; that is, a particular message through a particular messenger for a particular audience. Paul was from the beginning and is today a controversial figure who evokes admiration, devotion, and allegiance or disgust, hatred, and opposition.

If one feature of Paul's ministry stands out in contrast to the attitudes of today's preachers, it would be patience. Paul persevered in his total mission and in local expressions of that ministry. He generally took regions and cities one by one. The Acts narrative is sometimes interpreted in such a way as to suggest that the Apostle moved from successful revival to successful revival. When he left a city quickly it was under duress. Return trips for the purpose of confirmation and encouragement were common. He chose the important commercial, cultural, and communications centers from which a ripple effect would carry his message throughout the region. He spent eighteen months in Corinth (Acts 18:11) after having worked out of Damascus for two or three years (Gal. 1:18) and a similar period in Antioch. His tenure at Corinth explains the pastoral character of his correspondence with the church there. In many of the places he served he remained as long as many pastors remain on a church field. He was a resident pastor who preached with full awareness of the needs of a particular congregation. Wherever he went, he developed friendships and enlisted others who assisted him in the work and continued it after he departed. His letters are filled with affectionate allusions to fellow workers. There is a definite sense in which his preaching could be described as relational because he identified with people as fellow sinners, fellow workers, fellow Jews, and so forth. He went to where the people were and spoke to them in their own language.

Often his itinerary was determined by his opposition. There were always obstacles to be overcome. The physical and psychological abuse he suffered would have been more than enough to discourage a lesser person. Angrily he reviewed his sufferings for his critics at Corinth:

> Five times I have received at the hands of the Jews the forty lashes less one. Three times I have been beaten with rods; once I was stoned. Three times I have been shipwrecked; a night and a day I have been adrift at sea; on frequent journeys, in danger from rivers, danger from robbers, danger from my own people, danger from Gentiles, danger in the city, danger in the wilderness, danger at sea, danger from false brethren; in toil and hardship, through many a sleepless night, in hunger and thirst, often without food, in cold and exposure. And, apart from other things, there is the daily pressure upon me of my anxiety for all the churches. (2 Cor. 11:24-28)

This is not a bad passage for meditation for the pastor experiencing depression just because of the daily frustrations of shepherding. Paul's plans for his work were often interrupted by violent reaction to his preaching, misunderstanding, and even divine intervention. According to Luke, the Holy Spirit prevented the missionaries from going into Asia Minor, forbade them to go to Bithynia, and directed them in a dream to go to Macedonia (Acts 16:6-10). Paul always seemed to have a plan in mind but also could appropriately respond to spontaneous events and revelations.

Conclusion

Paul's early life prepared him for his special role in God's mission. After his call to the service of Christ, he continued to draw on his experiences recognizing that skills and knowledge are often a-moral and a-theological and that proper use invests virtue. Paul

48

Paul the Preacher

understood that his past should not be a chain that bound him but roots from which he could grow. He utilized the best Greek rhetoric, linguistic skills, literary and philosophical knowledge, and his Jewish heritage including his preparation to be a Pharisee to become a prototype preacher-missionary. Paul was one of the most learned and trained persons of his age, and he unashamedly used all of his gifts in the service of the Kingdom.

Notes

1. Martin Dibelius and Werner Georg Kummel, *Paul*, trans. Frank Clarke (Philadelphia: The Westminster Press, 1953), 10. Primary non-biblical sources for this chapter in addition to Dibelius are Gunther Bornkamm, *Paul* trans. D. M. G. Stalker, (New York: Harper and Row, 1972); David Smith, *The Life and Letters of St. Paul* (New York: Harper and Brothers, n.d.); J. S. Stewart, *A Man in Christ* (New York: Harper and Brothers, n.d.).

2. Stewart, 57.

3. Ibid.

4. Bornkamm, 12.

5. Stewart, 43.

6. Ibid., 44.

7. Dibelius, 37.

8. Smith, 34*ff.*

9. Dibelius, 36.

10. Acts 23:16 mentions "the son of Paul's sister," but a spouse or children are never indicated.

11. Bornkamm, 15.

12. Dibelius, 46. Bornkamm takes a similar position, "when Paul was converted, it was not the case of a man without faith finding the way to God, but of one zealous for God, more in earnest than anyone else about his demands and promises" (23).

13. The classical work on this aspect of Paul's experience and teaching is Albert Schweitzer, *The Mysticism of Paul the Apostle* (New York: Henry Holt and Company, 1931).

14. Some scholars argue that Galatians 2 corresponds with Acts 11 rather than Acts 15.

15. Krister Stendahl, *Paul Among Jews and Gentiles* (Philadelphia: Fortress Press, 1976), 43.

3

Revelation to Proclamation: Paul's Theology of Preaching

Christian preaching and theology are, or should be, indissoluble. Theology provides the rationale and context for preaching. Preaching in which psychology or moral instruction are preeminent is not Christian preaching. Christian ethics and Christian psychology should be rooted in and emerge from understanding God as creator and Lord.

Every Christian is a theologian; the question is whether one is a good theologian or a bad one. Preachers are charged with the responsibility of explaining and applying theology. The statement has often been made that Paul did not write theology and, if one has in mind speculative or systematic theology, there is some truth in the statement. Paul preached, however, because of his experience of God, and what he preached was based on his understanding of the will of God. The revelation of God in Jesus Christ was the why and what of the preaching of Paul as it should be for every preacher. Everything that Paul the missionary-preacher did emerged from his experience and understanding of God. His personal life and professional life were directed by his sense of the indwelling Spirit. No where did he express this more clearly than in the letter to the Galatians: "I have been crucified with Christ; it is no longer I who live, but Christ who lives in me . . . ." (Gal. 2:20).

The Lord Our God Is One

The words "Hear, O Israel: The Lord our God is one Lord; and you shall love the Lord your God with all your heart, and with all your soul, and with all your might" (Deut. 6:4) were indelibly etched into the soundtrack of Paul's mind. Every Jewish male would have heard those words over and over, and as a Pharisee Paul would have spoken them over and over. Long before he heard of Jesus, Paul was satisfied that there was only one God whom he sought to serve by studying, obeying, teaching, and protecting the law. He delighted in the law but was condemned by what he loved (Rom. 7:22). God who had given the law delivered those who were overwhelmed by it.

> "For God has done what the law, weakened by the flesh, could not do: sending his own Son in the likeness of sinful flesh and for sin, he condemned sin . . . that the just requirement of the law might be fulfilled . . . ." (Rom. 8:3-4).

Paul did not discover God for the first time in Christ. He was not converted from a false God to a true one. He did discover a fuller revelation of God. He understood that the justice of God demands the wrath of God. The revelation of Christ gave Paul a fuller understanding of the meaning of the law.

Sin, A Serious Matter

Sixteen times Paul wrote about wrath that accompanies sin and resistance to God's justice.

> By "the wrath" Paul means God's holy displeasure at sin. It is the eternal divine reaction against evil without which God would not be the moral Governor of the world. Paul thinks of it as both present and future. It is that divine aversion to evil and sin which, though active in the present time, will not reach its climax till the Judgment.[1]

Paul took sin seriously and believed that it required a radical cure. He was convinced, moreover, that none escaped the dreadful effects of sin (Rom. 3:9; 5:12; 11:32). The human condition resulted from poor theology, "for although they knew God they did not honor him or give thanks to him, but they became futile in their thinking and their senseless minds were darkened" (Rom. 1:21).

Sin was, in Paul's mind, a matter of broken relationship with God. "Sin involves coming short of the divine glory, descent to a lower plane than that for which man was destined; or as he puts it

. . . cut off from the life of God (Eph. 4:18)."[2] Sin corrupted the will, darkened the imagination, and confused the intellect (Eph. 4:17-18; Col. 1:21). Archibald Hunter agrees that Paul treated sin as a state-of-being rather than a series of violations of a moral code, but he makes the important observation that it results from *decision,* a basic decision about life that is "a positive and destructive principle or power, endemic in man (and woman) and enslaving him (or her) . . . so that to get Paul's full meaning, we have almost to spell it with a capital S."[3] The inevitable result of unresolved sin is death. Sin "reigned in death" (Rom. 5:21), "leads to death" (Rom. 6:16), earns death as its wage (Rom. 6:23), is "the sting of death" (1 Cor. 15:56). Paul constructed a syllogism depicting the human condition without Christ:

Sin brings death
All have sinned
All will die.

Paul believed that the human condition was desperate because all stood under the judgment of God. Paul warned all that "by your hard and impenitent heart you are storing up wrath for yourself on the day of wrath when God's righteous judgment will be revealed" (Rom. 2:5). But "God," Paul declared, "has not destined us for wrath, but to obtain salvation through our Lord Jesus Christ" (1 Thess. 5:9).

Our Lord Jesus Christ

This was the great truth God disclosed about Himself to Paul. The new factor in Paul's faith was the truth that, "God sent forth his son, born of woman" (Gal. 4:4). The coming of Christ challenged Jewish transactional theology. Salvation was not a human achievement. The law had not failed but humanity had failed to live by it. What could not be earned was offered as gift. It was this reality which formed the basis of Paul's new life and new work. He became a new creature in the midst of a new world coming into being because "in Christ God was reconciling the world to himself, not counting their trespasses against them, and entrusting to us the message of reconciliation" (2 Cor. 5:19).[4] Christians often err in stressing Paul's break with the past. Paul insisted on continuity between Judaism and Christianity. Paul, like Jesus and the original disciples, did not reject temple and synagogue; he was driven out. Christ was the fulfillment of God's covenant promises.

God exalted Jesus as Lord over all, the one who would hand over to God creation "set free from its bondage to decay" (Rom. 1:19-21; 1 Cor. 15:24; Rom. 15:16; 2 Cor. 2:14). Christ was the means of salvation from sin, the one through whom God did what the law could not do. Christ was the personification of the love of God from which no power could separate believers (Rom. 8:38-39). Jesus was the incarnation of God, Lord, and resurrected Lord. The symbol of death and life, the old and new creation, was Jesus' death and resurrection. The horror of sin was fully exposed in its effect on Christ. Christ bore sin in His innocence (Rom. 8:3; 4:25; 2 Cor. 5:21). Christ was the propitiation for sin, the redeemer and the reconciler (Rom. 3:24-25; 1 Cor. 5:7; Eph. 1:7; Titus 2:14).[5] Christ was the ransom, the mediator, the bridge between God and humanity; Paul was commissioned to declare that truth (1 Tim. 2:5-7). The resurrection was the warrant for all the rest; therefore, it was of "first importance" (1 Cor. 15:3). It further was the warrant for the hope of all believers because Jesus was "the first fruits of those who have fallen asleep" (1 Cor. 15:20*ff.*).

Justification by Faith

Krister Stendahl contends that Paul's emphasis was on justification by faith rather than forgiveness. His stress is on the new creature, the transformed person. Paul's major focus was on new life rather than past sin. Stendahl paraphrases Romans 1:17 to read "There will come a time when the righteous live by faith."[6] God's justification was the means of including all humankind. God's righteous act in Jesus Christ is making things right, putting all creation in order, and putting persons in right relationship to Him and to one another. Justification for Paul was more than mere forgiveness; it was the exposing of evil in the world that invoked God's wrath. Humans were lost even without knowledge of salvation because they lived a lie that produced a destructive life-style. Justification is the act by which we see the world and ourselves as we should be, God's plan of harmony for all creation. Justification puts the justified in right relationship to God and creation. In Christ, the inclusiveness of God, the common lostness and common potential salvation for Jews and Greeks is disclosed. Salvation is not just forgiveness but a new way of seeing and being in the world. Forgiveness has to do with the past, but justification has to do with the present and future. Forgiveness frees one to have a future in fellowship with God.

A New Age

Jesus marked the beginning of a new era. Hunter argues that Paul's preaching on this issue is a strong rebuttal to those who charged him with creating a new gospel different from the one Jesus proclaimed. Jesus began His ministry with the declaration that the Kingdom had come. Paul's preaching was in the context of the Kingdom age. His message was an eschatological one that stressed possibilities born with the kingdom in Christ. The power of the kingdom was the sign of the true gospel (1 Cor. 4:19-21). Believers were delivered "from the dominion of darkness . . . to the kingdom of his beloved Son" (Col. 1:13). The consummation of the work of Christ would be the defeat of evil and death and then "he [Christ] delivers the kingdom to God the father" (1 Cor. 15:20-28).

I said in Chapter 1 that Paul did not preach *like* Jesus and that is true, but he did *preach* Jesus. He preached Jesus the Christ who was dead and now lives.

Paul . . . looks back on the finished journey and all the blessings it brings with it . . . the discrepancy between Jesus and Paul is simply the difference of situations before and after Easter and Pentecost. What differentiates Paul and the first Christians from Jesus is that for them the New Age has come in power with the death, resurrection and exaltation of Jesus. With these events the period of the law is over . . . the righteousness of God has become a *fait accompli;* the new *Ecclesia* of God is a reality; the Holy Spirit has come; and

> Christians are . . . enjoying even now a foretaste of the perfected
> salvation of God.[7]

Jesus was not only revelation of the past and the present, He was also the revelation of the future. He anticipated the soon and physical return of Christ (1 Thess. 5:1-11; 2 Thess. 2:1-12; 1 Cor. 15:51*ff.*). Christians do not cease activity and retire to a shelter to wait for the final consummation because "whether we wake or sleep we might live with him" (1 Thess. 5:10). The special character of the church is explained in terms of its nature as an eschatological community. A part of the proclamation of Paul was new relationships among people that reflected the presence of the Spirit of God. Love, peace, and service were to dominate the Christian community (Rom. 12:10,16; 15:5,7; 14:13,19).[8]

Such a community could exist because believers were "God's temple . . . God's spirit dwells in you" (1 Cor. 3:16*ff.*). The Messianic age was the age of the Spirit. The gifts that made Christians different were gifts of the Spirit (Eph. 4:1*ff.*). We are made children of God through the Spirit (Rom. 8:15). The Holy Spirit is the instrument that energizes faith: "No one can say 'Jesus is Lord' except by the Holy Spirit" (1 Cor. 12:3).[9] The Spirit of God dwells in every Christian as the source of life and quality living (Rom. 8:9). The Spirit is God's continuing presence within believers guiding them in their living and even in their praying (Rom. 8:26-27).

Nowhere in the Bible does the word "trinity" appear. Paul did not enunciate such a doctrine but he did give a great deal of attention to the manifestations of the Spirit. He believed in God, Sovereign Lord of the universe, who was deeply involved in His creation. God disclosed Himself in Jesus Christ and empowered people through the Holy Spirit.

Law, Friend or Foe?

The law was the revelation of the righteousness of God that revealed the unrighteousness of humanity. Paul was not an enemy of the law for the law was a gift of God, but God revealed to him the limits of the law, its inadequacy with regard to salvation. It was a map that disclosed where the human race took the wrong road (Gal. 3:19; Rom. 7:7-12). The law was inert, a sign delivered by an intermediary (Gal. 3:19-20). The law delivered the sentence of death and held human conscience and spirit in custody (Gal. 3:23-25; 1 Tim. 1:8-11). God Himself came to reveal the tragedy of sin, the fatal flaw depriving humans of life, and to meet the demands of the law in His own suffering: "Christ redeemed us from the curse of the law . . . ." (Gal. 3:13). Paul preached the God of Abraham, Isaac and Jacob, but he also proclaimed the God and Father of the Lord Jesus Christ who energizes people through His Holy Spirit.

The Word of God

Paul had a great deal to say about preaching as an agency in God's plan of redemption. God who spoke the world into being speaks the word of regeneration. The gospel is not "the word of men but . . . the word of God, which is at work in you believers" (1 Thess. 2:13) calling a new world into being.

> Since it is "word" *(logos)*, it requires a voice! In the same way that Paul explains that the preaching of the gospel and living of the gospel must correspond to its message, to Christ (1:6), so also the medium of the gospel must correspond to the fact that it is the word of God. If the word is alive and creative, it requires a means of communication that is alive and creative. And that means is the human voice. The word is oral. The human voice calls forth an audience, and in the audience's hearing it has a direct, personal effect.[10]

Preaching at its best is not just about the word of God, it becomes the word of God for it "pleased God through the folly of what we preach to save those who believe" (1 Cor. 1:21). For Paul true gospel preaching was an event. The presence of the Holy Spirit makes something happen. Preaching is not reporting, but representing. Even Paul's language suggests action.

> The majority of references to *euaggelizesthai* and *euaggelion* which occur in the New Testament are found in the Pauline corpus. Paul's usage is derived from the Old Testament, especially from Deutero-Isaiah, where the two terms connote not only a message of

good news but an effective power (note that Isaiah 52:7 is quoted in Paul's important discussion of the gospel in Rom. 10:15).[11]

Paul referred to teachers as an office in the church only twice (1 Cor. 12:18; Eph. 4:11) and in each instance separated "apostles" and "prophets." Twice in the Pastoral Epistles he referred to himself as a teacher but each time alongside "preacher" and "apostle" (1 Tim. 2:7; 2 Tim. 1:11). He was first a preacher declaring the good news. Preaching was (and is) power unleashed by the Spirit through a servant of the Word. It cannot be managed by humans. Preaching is always more than the mere transfer of information.

Paul clearly conceived of himself as an apostle in function as well as position, that is, as "one sent" to evangelize the world (Rom. 1:1; Gal. 1:15). He interpreted his call as a specific one to carry the good news to the Gentiles (Acts 9:15, 26:17; Gal. 1:16; Rom. 15:16). He eventually concluded that he was to preach where no one else had proclaimed Christ (Rom. 15:20; 2 Cor. 10:15*ff.*). Preaching was his essential function as opposed to other pastoral functions, thus he boasted that he did not even baptize those who responded to his preaching (1 Cor. 1:17; 1 Tim. 2:5-7).

The importance of preaching in Paul's thought is expressed clearly in his discourse on the Israelites and the new covenant in Romans 9:11. Saving faith is elicited by preaching and preaching requires a preacher. The preacher is one who has been sent by God. "Faith comes from what is heard, and what is heard comes by the preaching of Christ" (Rom. 10:17). Paul was called upon to defend his apostleship on numerous occasions. He claimed that special authority that derived from having seen the Lord and having been personally called to service by Him. He counted himself among that select group of twelve, the best known of whom was Peter. However, Paul's use of the word apostle was not limited to the original select group. He identifies certain co-workers such as Silvanus, Timothy, Barnabas, and even Apollos as "apostles of Christ" (1 Cor. 4:9, 9:5; 1 Thess. 2:7). There were also counterfeit preachers who traveled about touting their own gifts and bearing letters of recommendation. They challenged Paul's credentials and declared themselves (like some today) "real" apostles and "servants of Christ" (2 Cor. 11:5,22; 12:11).[12] The irony of the situation was that Paul had come to them when apostolic authority meant nothing to them. He had come from another culture and religion to present the claims of the gospel. His message had been authenticated by its effects on their lives, but others had come to play word games with them and confuse them. The word of God is transmitted in saving power through those who are called and sent by God in the power of the Spirit. Not all those who claimed to have been sent were. The test is in the word that is proclaimed. The truth of God is, in the final analysis, self-authenticating. The word preached was more important in the mind of Paul than the person preaching. He was pleased when the truth was preached, even if for the wrong reasons (Phil. 1:12-18).

Receiving the Word

An important insight that Paul shares in the Romans 10 passage has to do with the responsibility of those who *hear* the word that is preached. This is a vital factor in preaching that is often overlooked by contemporary preachers. There is a limit on what the proclaimer can do. Response cannot be controlled. A called preacher can deliver in perfect form a word from the Lord that is perfectly understood and rejected. People cannot believe that which they have not heard and they hear through a called preacher (Rom. 10:14), but even when "the word is near . . . the word of faith which we preach" they must believe in their hearts and confess with their mouths (Rom. 10:8-10). Active listening is the order of the day for those within the sound range of revelation.

The responsibility of hearing was not an original theme with Paul. John the Baptizer spoke of the need to "accept" the message and "hear" intentionally (Matt. 11:13-15). Jesus echoed Israel's rebuke of the people who: "hear and hear, but do not understand; see and see, but do not perceive" (Isa. 6:9; Matt. 13:14-15). Jesus challenged His listeners time and again to "hear" (Mark 4:9,33; 7:14-16; Luke 8:8, 14:35).

Paul linked the new life to hearing and receiving the word of life. He gave thanks to God that the Thessalonians, "received the word of God which you heard from us" and "accepted it" as such (1 Thess. 2:13). He wrote the Colossians that the word of truth began to grow and bear fruit "from the day you heard and understood the grace of God in truth" (Col. 1:3-7). There must be someone who literally speaks the truth, but physical hearing is not enough.

The preacher must not only gain a physical hearing, but must strive to overcome psychological obstacles and find images and words with emotional tone and meaning that will produce understanding. Paul's primary Old Testament texts in this passage reminded him painfully that those who hear must act for the word to be effective. Hearers had to obey and in hope lay hold of the promise.

> Obedience means repentance; and repentance means prepardness to enter upon the divine, seasonable, eschatological possibility, to bow before the wrath and before the mercy of God, to be accessible to the one-sided, passionate, and exclusive claim which God makes upon men . . . . obedience means being committed to a particular course of action.[13]

Intellectual assent to the truth of a past action or to a theory is an insufficient response. The message requires action. Jerome Murphy O'Conner sums up Paul's teaching on the subject as follows:

> (1) Paul distinguishes "mere hearing" and "faith hearing."
> (2) "Mere-hearing," because of dispositions reducible to proud obstinacy, remains outside the religious sphere on the material level of aural sensation.
> (3) "Faith-hearing" is accompanied by genuine religious knowledge and is so closely bound up with faith as to be practically identifiable with it.[14]

Paul commonly used the language of acceptance to describe his own commitment to Christ (1 Cor. 11:23, 15:3; Gal. 1:12). He urged his followers to practice what they "received" from him (Phil. 4:9).[15] He often used "accepting Christ" as a synonym of "faith"; for example, Col. 2:6-7: "As therefore you received Christ Jesus the Lord, so live in him, rooted and built up in him and established in the faith . . . ." Paul understood, without benefit of communication theory, that communication is an act that requires a message being sent and received. He knew that he could not coerce belief in Jesus Christ but could only remove whatever obstacles might interfere with transmission of the truth. It was the realization that the word of salvation had to be received that generated "great sorrow and unceasing anguish" in his heart for his Jewish kinsfolk (Rom. 9:2). "It was not," he wrote, "as though the word of God had failed" (9:6). Contemporary preachers must work hard to remove the barriers that obstruct "hearing" the gospel but they also must realize that they can do everything right and still people may not "receive" the word. The preacher cannot always assume responsibility for the refusal to hear, the rejection of the gospel. These thoughts motivated Paul's impassioned plea for preachers to proclaim the truth (10:8-21).

This element in Paul's theology has too often been neglected and has produced some preaching aberrations that have victimized people and compromised authentic Christian proclamation. No psychological manipulation, coerced confessions, or commitments based on false promises can result in genuine conversion. Circus attractions may gather a crowd, and public humiliation may get people down an aisle, but such tricks and deceptions cannot transform the human mind and life. Salvation is an event that occurs in God's time in the context of the church and in the power of the Spirit. Preachers must treat preaching with great seriousness but must guard against taking themselves too seriously.

Acceptance of the word of truth is acceptance of God's trustworthiness and of His gift of righteousness. Jews and Gentiles alike are "justified by his grace as a gift, through the redemption which is in Christ Jesus" (Rom. 3:24). This gift is appropriated by faith (Rom. 3:26). Faith, for Paul, was trust in God's word and God's act. Faith as a noun appears nearly 200 times in Pauline literature. Faith meant more than intellectual assent to Paul, it meant the risk of obedience to the dominance of love in all relationships, a commitment to a community, values different from those of most of society.[16] Faith for Christians was different than faith for the Pharisees, who trusted a written code as the final word of God and their ability to fulfill that code. Christians, on the other hand, trusted the work of God in Christ, that is, their confidence was in a person rather than in propositions. Faith according to Paul was more than a pledge or a single act, it was a way of viewing the world and a life-style. Galatians 2:20 summarizes the faith that Paul preached: "I have been crucified with Christ; it is no longer I who live, but Christ who lives in me; and the life I now live in the flesh I live by faith in the son of God, who loves me and gave himself for me" (2:20).

The Word Happening

Paul believed that preaching the gospel is a part of God's strategy for bringing women and men to salvation. It is not a possibility but a necessity for transmitting the gospel. It is not just a report on something that happened; it is a happening, an event in which the Holy Spirit is active. A preacher is called by God as an instrument of God's "yes." Preaching is aimed at re-presenting the Christ who is the full revelation of God.

Summary

Preaching involves four essential elements: God, the message, the preacher, and the audience. For preaching to achieve its purpose of evoking saving faith, all four must fulfill a function. Daniel Patte has constructed four theses to characterize Paul's functional theology of preaching. These theses provide a suitable matrix for the application of Paul's theology of preaching.

Thesis I
The proclamation of the word (kerygma) is *necessary,* indeed *essential* (Romans 10), for the transmission of the gospel, that is, for the transmission and the nurture of the Christian faith, but it is *not sufficient.*[17]

Patte joins others mentioned above and distinguishes the Greek verbs *kerysso* and *euaggelizo,* the former meaning merely "to proclaim," the latter "to transmit." We discussed earlier Paul's preference for *euaggelizo* stressing that the message must be received. The act of preaching is not a sacrament in the medieval sense of the act itself conveying grace. The word is not mysteriously or magically transferred to those present simply because it is true and the preacher is inspired. There must be a faith response that apprehends the message and submits to the God who has revealed Himself in the message.

Thesis 2
The proclamation of the Word is *not sufficient* for the transmission of the gospel because the gospel is for Paul "the power of God for salvation" (Rom. 1:16). The gospel involves manifestations of the power of God. Without manifestations of God, the message or Word is powerless.

The Holy Spirit is active in the preaching event, bearing testimony in the words, through the preacher, and within the hearer. Again, something happens. Patte concludes that the historical manifestation in Jesus and the manifestation in the preaching process are necessary but not enough. God must be present in the experience of the hearers for the word to effect transformation. Patte cautions that preachers cannot wash their hands and deny responsibility in this realm. The ministry of the preacher as well as the proclamation may serve to obstruct or remove obstructions to the experience of God. The preacher can, moreover, assist the hearer in recognizing God's work when it might otherwise be misunderstood and labeled incorrectly. It is important, however, to understand that the preacher does not make something happen but explains what is happening as a result of God's action. Paul's message interpreted history, nature, and human experience through the microscope of divine revelation to set free signs of God's activity that were there all the time. The modern preacher cannot ignore truth no matter what its source.

Thesis 3
The proclamation of the message of the gospel is *the proclama-*

tion of a promise . . . that through Christ God has reconciled the world to himself . . . that, after Christ, God does intervene in human affairs . . . .

The proclamation of the gospel announced a new age of hope in which faith is possible (Gal. 3:22-25). The hearer is invited to believe in the promise that reconciliation with God and with the world occurs in Jesus Christ. The believer lives with confident expectation that God's promises are being fulfilled. "Faith is trusting that God intervened in Christ, but it is also taking hold of God's promise and looking for, and indeed seeing, God at work in our experience and, of course, acting accordingly."[18]

Thesis 4

The proclamation of the gospel as the "power of God for salvation" involves both the proclamation of the Word/message/promise *AND* the proclamation of how and when God intervenes in the hearers' experience. When preaching does not proclaim such fulfillment of the promise of the gospel, it is unwittingly conveying a belief in justification through works instead of a belief in justification through faith.

Preaching is not the mere transfer of information, it is a "demonstration of the Spirit and of power" that succeeds when it results in the power of God being received and lived (1 Cor. 2:3-5). There is a critical difference in knowing about God and the historical Jesus and knowing God and the resurrected Christ. Unwittingly, we sometimes preach a doctrine of salvation through works that makes demands rather than offering the gift of grace. Paul proclaimed the power and work of the Spirit and offered insight into how God is working now. God is working for us, in us, and through us. A major portion of his preaching was devoted to interpreting what God was doing in the world. He gave form to deep human feelings and exegeted them through the revelation of God as he was experiencing it. The preacher points out what God has done and what He will do. The power to see and to live according to God's plan for life depends on appropriation of the living Word by faith.

63

Revelation to Proclamation: Paul's Theology of Preaching

Notes

1. Archibald M. Hunter, *The Gospel According to St. Paul* (Philadelphia: The Westminster Press, 1966), 71.

2. C. A. Anderson Scott, *Christianity According to St. Paul* (London: Cambridge Press, 1966), 48.

3. Hunter, 17; cf. Dibelius, 113*ff.*

4. See Schweitzer, 112*ff.*

5. Jerome Murphy O'Conner, *Paul on Preaching* (New York: Sheed and Ward, 1963), 12.

6. Stendahl, 20.

7. Hunter, 79.

8. Robin Scroggs, *Paul for a New Day* (Philadelphia: Fortress Press, 1977), 39*ff.*

9. See Murphy O'Conner, 115*ff;* cf. Bornkamm, 180*ff.*

10. Beaudean, 56.

11. Ibid., 36; cf. Murphy O'Conner, 167-87, and David Patte, *Preaching Paul* (Philadelphia: Fortress Press, 1984), 23.

12. Bornkamm, 74.

13. Murphy O'Conner, 222.

14. Karl Barth, *The Epistle to the Romans,* trans. Edwyn C. Hoskyns (New York: Oxford University Press, 1968), 386.

15. Ibid., 226.

16. Hunter lists five characteristics of Pauline faith, 27-28.

17. Patte, the four theses and explanation are found on 21-30. Italics added.

18. Ibid., 26-27.

4

The Urbanization of the Gospel

Paul did not imitate the preaching of Jesus; that is, he did not imitate the form of his Lord's preaching. He did, however, follow the example of Jesus in strategizing to reach a particular audience. He shaped his message for specific audiences, just as Jesus did. He identified with those he served, but because the groups served were different, the forms of identification differed. Paul preached in a different time a message that had an added component. The death and resurrection of Jesus marked a new stage in God's plan of redemption. The central point in Paul's message was that the resurrection was sufficient warrant for trust in all that Jesus had said and was the key to understanding His person.

Jesus addressed Jews, usually in rural environments. He shared with them the common bonds of ethnicity, culture, and knowledge of and respect for the Old Testament. Paul, on the other hand, preached to Gentiles with only a general education in common. Jesus relied almost all together on narration. Paul resorted to logic, appeal to authority, and, occasionally, abstract reasoning. These dissimilarities should not distract from the fundamental principles which informed the preaching of each. Each adapted the message to the needs and nature of his target group. The forms which each employed were appropriate to his respective situation, to God's purpose for him, and the particular stage of development of God's plan for the world.

Illustrations were selected for their potential impact on a particular audience. Jesus talked about birds, mustard seeds, sowing and reaping, sheep and shepherds, bread and fish, tares and wheat. Paul's analogies were based on Greek athletic competition, military life, the body, and experiences common to living in an urban, pluralistic society. Each worked from the known to the unknown, the familiar to the unfamiliar. They used different forms but had a common strategy, to make the message understandable and attractive without compromising the integrity of message, speaker, or audience. Language that was meaningful for the hearers was used. Each preacher went to where his audience was, identified with them, and addressed their needs. The message was particularized for the moment. The so-called particularity of the gospel extends beyond the sense of embodiment in the person Jesus; each preaching mission should represent particularity. Bornkamm notes that Paul's epistles "do not move in the realm of abstract, theoretical reflection, but always include the hearers' actual situations as a determining factor."[1] The same may be said of Jesus.

A Matter of Ethics

Paul's great respect for his audience as persons created by God and for whom Christ died would not allow him to use deceptive tactics to attract them or persuade them.[2] Method was as pure as message. While he employed the best of Greek rhetoric, he did not stoop to the manipulation of the sophists who would use eloquent language to confuse rather than clarify thought. He also differed from the sophists in that his skill could not be bought. He did not change the essence of his message to accommodate the tastes and life-styles of the wealthy and influential. Paul used different forms to achieve clarity but not to soften demand or placate those for whom the cross was an offense. The traveling orators could be hired to speak on any side of an issue. They were more concerned with profit and acceptance than with truth. Some contemporary preachers become spokespersons for the status quo and defenders of social standards that are in conflict with the gospel in order to live comfortable lives. Paul refused to compromise the message or the form of the gospel. He knew the difference between good-sounding reason and sound reasoning (1 Cor. 2:3-5). Paul made no attempt to bribe or trick people into the kingdom of God.

Paul used strong language in disdaining the methods used by unethical adversaries. Paul lashed out at those who had seduced the minds of the people of Corinth calling them "peddlers of

God's word." He believed that many had preached a self-serving gospel but assured the Thessalonians that his appeal was free from "guile" and untainted by error or immorality (1 Thess. 2:3). He was determined to preach what people needed to hear rather than what would make him popular: "We speak not to please men, but to please God . . . we never used words of flattery . . . or a cloak for greed" (1 Thess. 2:4-5). He stated his rhetorical ethic clearly in the Corinthian correspondence:

> We have renounced disgraceful, underhanded ways; we refuse to practice cunning or to tamper with God's word, but by the open statement of the truth we would commend ourselves to every man's conscience in the sight of God (2 Cor. 4:2).

Most of us want to be loved or at least admired; there is a great temptation to preach those things that please people and win their approval. Paul did not want to be stoned, beaten, cursed, or jailed; but he would not compromise the integrity of his mission for personal security or approval. The spiritual, psychological and physical well-being of his audience was paramount to him.

He was honest about himself and his own struggles in the faith and was not reluctant to use himself as an example of one who needed the grace of God (1 Tim. 1:15-16). Paul's standard for his preaching was as high as it was for his personal life. He wanted the word he preached to be unadulterated (Titus 3:9) and the form to be worthy of the content. He was convinced that his language and argument should reflect an artistic effort that would honor and glorify God (2 Cor. 1:12; 1 Thess. 2:4). As we shall see in the chapters that follow, Paul appealed to the whole person. He used all the historical and factual data available to him, the best of human logic and appeal to value and feeling, but all with the greatest respect for truth and the dignity of individuals and their cultures. The rhetoric of Paul is free from cheap sentiment or emotional manipulation. Threat rarely rears its ugly head in his preaching, but when it does appear it is directed toward those who would distort the gospel or undermine the Christian mission. He did not use physical or psychological coercion as tools of persuasion.

An Urban Strategy

A study of Paul's work, what used to be called the missionary journeys, reflects an urban strategy.[3] The apostle wrote to the Romans of the geographical arc of his work: "from Jerusalem and as far round as Illyricum I have fully preached the gospel of Christ" (Rom. 15:19). Illyricum was a Roman province on the Adriatic Sea. It is unclear as to whether Paul actually preached in the province or noted it only as the western boundary on his excursion into Macedonia. Paul denied starting his ministry at Jerusalem (Gal. 1:17-24), but he may well have personally dated his most productive period from the Jerusalem Council. He may have chosen these geographical points as representing the theological and ethnic poles of his evangelistic efforts. Paul's home base and an early environment that surely shaped his ministry was Antioch of Syria.

Antioch

Antioch was the third largest city in the Roman Empire. It was a trade, intellectual, and cultural center. The population of this free city was estimated at half a million including a significant Jewish settlement. A well-established Christian church developed out of the work of those who had heard Stephen preach, responded to the martyr's message, and returned home to share it (Acts 11:19-20). The Jewish Christians had reached out to Greeks and many had turned to the Lord. The success at Antioch had come to the attention of those in Jerusalem who sent Barnabas to see what was going on there. He was so impressed that he remained and went to Tarsus to solicit Paul's assistance (Acts 11:19-26). The base of Paul's ministry was a Gentile-dominated church in a pluralistic metropolis. It was an ideal environment for the nurture of one who would be the apostle to the Gentiles. It was there that the conflict between Jewish tradition and Christian freedom erupted. This issue was circumcision with the entire Jewish code of dietary and social codes at stake by implication (Acts 15; Gal. 2).[4] The issue was resolved in favor of the freedom of Christians, but the peace was short-lived (Gal. 2:11-13). Paul continued to be plagued

Paul the Preacher

by the Judaizers who sought to exercise authority over him and Gentile converts. The events at Antioch and subsequently in Jerusalem gave him confidence in his understanding of Christian freedom and a sense of liberty with regard to the authority of others. Paul refused to accept hierarchical authority of one community over another. This position was important to the freedom of his preaching and to the development of the nature of the association of churches. Paul taught love and respect among churches and common submission to the Lordship of Christ, but never indicated that one church was over another in a political sense. He claimed personal authority based on the Holy Spirit's leadership, Scripture, truth tested and proved, and mutual love.

Nerve Centers

Paul's most productive work was centered in the Roman provinces of Galatia, Asia, Macedonia, and Achaia. In those regions he concentrated his efforts in cities of influence like Antioch where he began. The cities were on the rise in number and influence. Agriculture was the base of the economy, but the ownership of the land was increasingly in the hands of entrepreneurs who preferred to live in the cities and conduct their business from there. Cities were the nerve centers for all of life. The cities were where manners and customs were formed.

> The city . . . was the place where the new civilization could be experienced, where novelties would first be encountered. It was the place where . . . change could be met and even sought out. It was where the empire was, and where the future began.[5]

The city provided an environment where new ideas could be heard, tested, and accepted. The cities that are prominent in Pauline correspondence were centers of commerce, affecting thought and life not only in the areas surrounding them but in trade centers around the world. People came to the centers for business and pleasure and returned to tell the folks at home what were the latest ideas. Many who came under the preaching of Paul returned home with a new vision of reality and a message of salvation.

The Urbanization of the Gospel

Luke's chronicle of Paul's travels describes the Apostle's pattern of operation. Paul and his companions would go to the synagogue or other gathering places of Jews and exercise their right as Jewish males to preach and debate the Scriptures (Acts 16:11*ff.*; 17:1*ff.*, 10; 18:4-19; 19:8). Paul was a Jew who stressed the continuity of God's revelation. He went to his fellow religionists and ethnics first, but Paul and his colleagues were rarely well received among the Jewish faithful. They often met with rejection and sometimes violence (Acts 17:5-9; 18:6,12; 19:9). Driving Paul out of the synagogues did not silence him. He preached anywhere people would listen. He spoke in private homes, jail cells, or public forums. He took advantage of public hearings to proclaim the truth entrusted to him (Acts 13:7-12; 16:25-31; 21:37*ff.*; 22:30*ff.*; 25:6-12). He adapted himself to the situation and spoke appropriately to gain a hearing. He demonstrated respect and courtesy before officials and dialogued with scholars on their own terms. His was rarely a take-it-or-leave-it attitude or manner.

Paul first sought out fellow Jews to share the good news of the Messiah. Not unlike contemporary cities in the United States, cities contained ethnic neighborhoods that could be located with some ease. As Chinese, Polish, Italian, and Black communities can be found in cities like Los Angeles, Chicago, and New York, Paul could find the Jewish ghetto in Ephesus, Corinth, and Laodicea. Cities would also be marked off in trade zones[6] and Paul sometimes began with fellow crafts workers. He did not have to have a crowd to bear witness to his experience with Christ. The newly established churches met in private homes. These homes were often places where Paul had found hospitality from new friends and converts, such homes as those of Lydia (Acts 16:15), Jason (Acts 17:5-9), Priscilla and Aquila (Acts 18:2-4), of Titus Justus (Acts 18:7). He made new friends and developed relationships that became agencies for transmitting the gospel. Paul pioneered the practice of life-style evangelism. He spent the necessary time to develop relationships that would produce not only converts but missionaries.

A Diverse Audience

Celsus, a second-century critic of Christianity, charged that Christianity was a stupid religion that could appeal only to the ignorant. "The Christian evangelists," he said, "were wool-workers, cobblers, laundry workers, and the most illiterate and bucolic yokels, who enticed 'children . . . and stupid women' . . . ."[7] Such an assessment was certainly not true of Celsus' time, when such thinkers as Tertullian and Clement were soon to be followed by even more powerful thinkers like Origen who produced a systematic theology.[8] Some scholars have identified Paul with the lower classes in spite of his Roman citizenship and literary powers, but Meeks's analysis of those Paul mentions in his writings concludes that the early church included a cross-section of the general society.[9] He interprets the evidence to infer that Pauline Christianity was primarily middle-class in social orientation. There was a social mix ranging from the upper lower class to the lower upper class. There were wealthy and poor, educated and uneducated.

> A Pauline congregation generally reflected a fair cross-section of urban society. Moreover, those persons prominent enough in the mission or in the local community for their names to be mentioned . . . exhibit signs of a high ranking in one or more dimensions of status. But that is typically accompanied by low rankings in other dimensions . . . the most active and prominent members of Paul's circle . . . are people of high status inconsistency. They are upwardly mobile; their achieved status is higher than their attributed status.[10]

This analysis would explain the assertive institutionalization of Christianity and aggressive evangelism. They were the kind of people who were not easily satisfied and who made things happen. There is no evidence that Paul or his companions made any effort to establish homogeneous congregations. He chided those who would create divisions among Christians. Paul preached "one body," "one Spirit," "one faith," "one baptism" (Eph. 4:1-6). It is difficult to imagine Paul encouraging color-coded congregations or communities based on socio-economic standards.

The Urbanization of the Gospel

We know that his disciples included merchants, persons with houses large enough to accommodate services, free persons and slaves, people with enough money to travel.[11] Diversity is evident in some of the early conflicts in the church. Paul spoke harshly of the divisions at Corinth (11:17-34) which had developed along class lines. The gospel was intended to break down walls of social status and economics no less than walls of race and nationality.

Corinth

The great cities shared some strengths and weaknesses common to urban life, but they were by no means all alike. Cities in that day as in our own had distinctive characters—personalities that required different evangelistic approaches. Two such cities were Corinth and Ephesus.

Corinth was the southernmost stop on Paul's journey to Greece. It was a center of commerce known for its wealth. Destroyed in 146, the city was a model Roman city, a city without landed gentry, a city filled with opportunity for the upwardly mobile. There were no long-established families who controlled growth and thought. The city was known for the priestesses who served the Temple of Aphrodite. Corinth was notorious for sexual immorality promoted as religious ritual. Sailors often paid for their pleasures with diseases they carried home with them.[12]

Corinth was highly regarded for handicrafts. Paul made his initial contacts in the city through his craft. His attempts to persuade the Jews and Greek proselytes in synagogue debate were unsuccessful and he turned to Gentiles. He was joined in his efforts by Titus Justus, a God-believer, and Crispus the president of the synagogue (Acts 18:4-11). Paul labored in Corinth for eighteen months. He became a resident pastor whose sermons undoubtedly applied Christian faith to everyday problems. At Corinth, he spoke of "a secret and hidden wisdom of God" (1 Cor. 2:7). He lived among them an exemplary life and reasoned with them about the spiritual. The work of the Spirit was a central theme of his preaching in Corinth. In the midst of a materialistic culture obsessed with pleasure and profit, Paul preached Jesus the crucified

Lord (1 Cor. 2:1-4). While the Corinthian correspondence indicates that the Christians there were not all of the same social economic level, a major segment seems to have been among those who would have been considered failures in that success-oriented society. Paul reminded them during their conflict that few of them "were powerful" or "of noble birth" (1 Cor. 1:26). He, like Jesus, had gone to where the people were and addressed them in terms they could understand about a salvation they needed. We'll look at specific Pauline rhetorical techniques in the next chapter.

Ephesus

Ephesus was, like Corinth, a prosperous city with all of the attractions of a great urban area. There were outstanding schools, beautiful art, eloquent statesmen, and wise philosophers. The city was a free city, the capital of Asia, renowned for literature and art. The Temple of Artemis located in the city was ranked as one of the Seven Wonders of the ancient world. The environs of the Temple were a legal sanctuary that offered asylum to criminals. Pilgrims were attracted as worshipers and as sightseers to this metropolis. The booming souvenir business supported a lucrative guild of silver artisans. The religion was one of prosperity and healing, selling lucky charms and mystical cures for human ills.[13] The city was home to the eloquent Apollos, an Alexandrian who followed John the Baptist, who "taught accurately the things concerning Jesus," and who was instructed by Priscilla and Aquila. When Paul arrived in Ephesus, Apollos went to Corinth (Acts 18:24—19:1). When Paul established his work at Ephesus, he stayed there for three years and made this famous pagan city a center for Christian ministry (Acts 19:1, 20:1; 20:31).

Paul challenged the charms and potion industry at Ephesus with a healing ministry that resulted in many converts from the magical cults (Acts 19:11-20). He used the resources that God had given him to meet the needs of the people and expose the weaknesses of false religions. After the Apostle was rejected by the Jews and driven out of the synagogue, he set up shop in a public hall where for two years he discussed and debated the gospel (Acts

The Urbanization of the Gospel

19:9-10). Preaching will have an impact on politics and economics and sometimes will result in violent reaction. Paul's preaching had a material effect on the business of the silversmiths and aroused a revolt among those who were economically threatened. The riot which followed forced Paul's withdrawal from the city.

A Strategy for Today

Paul preached the gospel in synagogue, marketplace, homes, rented halls—wherever he could gather a crowd. He did not shy away from dialogue with other religions and was not afraid to engage thinkers and leaders. He remained firm in his proclamation even when physically threatened but knew when withdrawal was in the best interests of his mission. He conversed with individuals and groups, discussed and debated, and delivered speeches when the occasion dictated. He worked with his hands, cooperated with other Christians, healed, and used every means available to him for sharing his faith. He demonstrated that for him preaching was determined by content rather than form.

Paul's urban strategy is one that should be studied carefully and perhaps adopted as a model for modern evangelism. The secular culture of Western civilization is similar in a number of ways to that of the first century. Leslie Newbiggin, a respected missiologist, theologian, former Bishop of Madras for the Church of South India and Director of World Mission and Evangelism for the World Council of Churches, wrote an article a few years ago, entitled "Can the West be Converted?" Hardly anyone in the United States would deny that the country is a highly pluralistic society with a plethora of competing philosophies and value systems. Like Corinth and Ephesus, the United States prides itself on its diversity and freedom of thought and expression. Certainly Paul's technique is worthy of emulation in any metropolitan city around the world. We do well to note that Paul did not evade the urban centers where intellectual debate, shaping of culture, and political activity took place; neither did he strive to establish safety islands within the cities that would encourage escape from secular society.

He penetrated the nerve centers of the cities and confronted the powerful and wise.

Print and electronic media provide ample evidence that our cities abound with people "telling or hearing something new" (Acts 17:21). Martin Marty reported that a recent conference in the nation's capitol included something for everyone. Programs included "The Path of Transformation in Meditation," "Journeying with the Christian Mystics," "Zen Dance: Meditation in Movement," "Chakra Psychology" and "Japanese Tea Ceremony as Ritual."[14] Scan the headlines of the tattler magazines at the checkout counter in your local pharmacy or grocery and observe the weird stories that sell magazines. Fortunes are made on books revealing the latest fantasies of movie stars.

Our cities and culture are like the ancient secular societies in harboring people fascinated with religion. Religion can be an obstacle to true faith, but it also can be the basis for sharing faith. Paul found in other religions a basis for conversation leading to disclosure of resurrection faith. The signs are everywhere in our society that people are driven by a religious impulse to seek God. The rise of cults and the success of Eastern religions and philosophies are just part of the evidence. In February 1989, an article in *New York Times Book Review* by novelist Dan Wakefield noted "a growing number of new literary works in which God . . . has returned as a force" or a "character" in the action.[15] Even scientists are entertaining new theories of creation that provide a gambit for discussion.

The effect of Paul's preaching was multiplied many times over because he focused on centers of culture, commerce, and learning. He worked in transportation and communication centers from where the gospel was naturally spread. Villages would have been easier places of service but would not have provided a platform for the world as the urban centers did.

Notes

1. Bornkamm, xxiv.

2. For a discussion of ethics in contemporary preaching, see Raymond Bailey, "Ethics in Preaching," *Review and Expositor* 86 (Fall 1989): 533-56.

3. Wayne A. Meeks, *The First Urban Christians: The Social World of the Apostle Paul* (New Haven: Yale University Press, 1983) provides an excellent survey of the literature on this subject and is the major source for much of the material in this chapter.

4. The Acts account indicates that James led the Council to decide in favor of the Antiochenes and sent an embassy to deliver their decision to the church (Acts 15:13-30). Paul's account in Galatians (2:1-10) suggests only that there was mutual agreement and a request from the Jerusalem church for an offering for the poor. Paul then records a confrontation between Peter and himself over attempts of a delegation from James seeking to impose Jewish restrictions on the Greeks.

5. Meeks, 15-16.

6. Ibid., 26.

7. Ibid., 31.

8. Williston Walker, *A History of the Christian Church* (New York: Charles Scribner's Sons, 1959), 72*ff.*

9. Meeks, 55*ff.*

10. Ibid., 73.

11. Ibid., 48.

12. Smith, 150.

13. Ibid., 224*ff.*

14. Martin Marty, "Worship Demands," *Christian Century*, January 24, 1990, 87.

15. Dan Wakefield, "And Now, a Word from Our Creator," *New York Times Book Review* (Feb. 12, 1989), 2.

5

The Rhetoric of Paul

Greek rhetoric was a part of Paul's heritage as a Roman citizen reared in a Hellenistic culture. Pauline literature is replete with examples of classical technique acquired by observation or intentional study but skillfully applied to the evangelistic task first, and then to the nurturing one. Paul had no formal political or ecclesiastical power. His only special social status was that he was a Roman citizen. His Roman citizenship helped him on several occasions in legal matters but contributed nothing to his persuasive efforts for the Gospel and Christian conduct. Paul, like Jesus before him, had to earn a hearing through personal conduct and the inherent power of his message. He had to work to establish credibility with his audiences. Paul could not set up shop, hang out a sign, and wait for the crowds. No revival promotion, promise of biblical preaching, or celebrity singers would attract a crowd.

When Paul became a Christian he did not repudiate his past as much as he baptized it. His knowledge of the sacred writings of the Hebrews (the Old Testament), his knowledge of the Greek language, his training as a Pharisee and in the rabbinic school (particularly with regard to exegesis), his travels and knowledge of cities, and his familiarity with Greek literature and culture were all harnessed in the service of the gospel. He used all the knowledge and skill at his disposal.

The Person of the Preacher

The perceived character of the advocate is of primary importance in any transaction involving value, but it is especially significant in religious matters—those that promote a religion or advocate a life-style. Christian preachers ask believers to make personal sacrifices and adhere to a demanding moral code that often puts them at odds with their culture. Skeptics investigate the lives of preachers to see if they conform to the standards they urge others to adopt. People are not likely to trust the words, the life principles, of persons they deem untrustworthy. People do not follow abstract philosophies or grand principles; they follow other people whose lives reflect principles that make life better. All the major world religions are linked to powerful founder figures. Moses, Confucius, and Mohammed each had to give evidence of special gifts and insights. Jesus had to establish personal credibility and so did Paul. The apostle was never able completely to escape the critics. He worked continually to win acceptance and defended himself against those who would undermine confidence once he won it.

Paul took no shortcuts for fear that he would compromise his integrity. He refused amenities to which he believed he was rightfully entitled because he did not want to be accused of preaching for the money. Wandering sophists, willing to speak on any subject or represent any cause for money, had long been a part of Greco-Roman culture. Itinerant preachers and sorcerer-magicians like Simon (Acts 8:9-24) were a common sight in Palestine.[1] Paul resisted the very appearance of evil.

Paul may have originated the confessional sermon. The Epistles (and the Pauline speeches in Acts) are replete with first-person pronouns. There is a school of homiletical thought today that discourages all personal references in a sermon. Paul's preaching would be totally unacceptable to those in that school because he used himself as an example, shared his history, confessed his sins, and disclosed personal religious experiences. The Bible as a record of revelation is a collection of testimonies about what God has done for people through persons. People are interested in other people and particularly people with whom they can identify. People are more likely to listen to the counsel of individuals who have had to cope with the same temptations, struggle with natural and human forces, and who have found a way to overcome.

Paul told his audience that he was a sinner, indeed "the fore-most of sinners" (1 Tim. 1:15), who had experienced the forgive-ness of God through Christ. Not only was he a sinner who felt forgiven, but he was also a Christian who continued to struggle with sin; "For I do not do what I want, but I do the very thing I hate" (Rom. 7:15). He testified to the law of human nature, "I find it to be a law that when I want to do right, evil lies close at hand" (Rom. 7:21). Paul's weakness was not limited to thorns in the flesh. He fought psychological and spiritual battles common to humanity. He did not deny human impulse or the difficulty of controlling thought and deed. He identified with Jews and Gen-tiles as a human being who had sinned and who had to resist temp-tation daily. He did not pretend to live above the fray. Paul let his audience know that he stood beside them.

Paul identified with his ministry group by living among them and earning his living with his hands. At Corinth he met Aquila and Priscilla and "stayed with them, and they worked, for by trade they were tentmakers" (Acts 18:3). Paul's action would be consid-ered by many observers to be a waste of time and energy that could have been spent in ministry. Paul knew that his image and his identification were of great importance to his mission. His inde-pendence was a rhetorical tool in the initial stages of his contact with particular groups and in later pastoral relationships. In 1 Co-rinthians 9, Paul eloquently presented the case for a paid ministry and immediately proceeded to remind them that he was free of any human obligation because he had made the gospel "free of charge" (9:18). Unfortunately, his efforts to avoid criticism have invited criticism of others who accept stipends to which they are entitled. Some modern Christians use these passages to justify poverty for contemporary clergy. The lesson may be that no matter which course one takes, someone will find fault. Paul knew what it was to live in poverty and plenty. He could speak to the human condition from experience. "I know how to be abased, and I know how to abound; in any and all circumstances I have learned the secret of facing plenty and hunger, abundance and want" (Phil. 4:12). He was with the people socially and economically.

The Rhetoric of Paul

Physical weakness and pain was another experience he had in common with believers and unbelievers alike. Paul could encourage others to endure suffering and joyfully live in hope in spite of pain because this was his own fate. He earned the greater respect and obedience of the Philippians by writing an epistle of joy while languishing in prison, facing possible execution. His indulgence of those who preached out of selfish motives gave credence to his admonition that they should make love the highest virtue. Those who had to endure chronic pain could not excuse themselves with complaints that the preacher just didn't know what they had to endure. Paul told the Corinthians of the thorn in his flesh (2 Cor. 7*ff.*). Here was a great man of faith specially called and blessed, occasionally manifesting extraordinary powers, and yet his affliction was not removed. He identified with people and he told them of the points of identification. Frequent use of "you," "we," "I," and "us" gave his message the sound of conversation between friends about common concerns.

Much has been made of the debate over Paul's apostleship. He was extremely defensive about this issue and frequently included in an epistle an apology for the authority of the apostolic office. Apparently there were two categories of apostles. Paul mocked the "superlative apostles" (2 Cor. 11:5,13; 12:11) who had seduced many of the Corinthians and created serious division. The implication is that there were apostles (persons sent out) other than the twelve and Paul. Apostles in the purest sense in the early church were those persons who had been personally appointed by Christ and had been with Him before the crucifixion.[2] Paul insisted that he had the appropriate credentials: ". . . the gospel which was preached by me is not man's gospel. For I did not receive it from man, nor was I taught it, but it came through a revelation of Jesus Christ" (Gal. 1:11-12). This was a theme repeated over and over in his writings (Rom. 1:1, 11:13; 1 Cor. 1:1; 2 Cor. 1:1; Eph. 1:1). He pleaded that he be judged by the truth of his words and the character of his works. He responded to his adversaries at Corinth with a call to remember his acts among them: "The signs of a true apostle were performed among you in all patience, with signs and wonders and mighty works" (2 Cor. 12:12).

Paul worked hard to win and maintain the trust of those he sought to lead to Christ. He set a good example for modern preachers who too often rely on position for authority or who are indifferent to the obstacles of personal distrust that impede the communication of the gospel. Preachers must do all in their power to convince the audience that they are knowledgeable, trustworthy, and have the audience's best interests uppermost in their goals.

The Gospel Particularized

Plato, who did not trust public speakers or the art of rhetoric, said that if there could be an advocate with integrity, he or she would have to know the souls of those to be persuaded.[3] He had in mind a philosophical understanding of human nature but others have recognized the importance of understanding a particular group. A preacher must understand people in order to identify with them and to appeal to those things about which they feel deeply. Paul's tenure in various locales allowed him to particularize his extraordinary insight into human nature. He was a perceptive student of human nature who not only reflected on his personal experience but on his observation of others as well. He never seems to have fallen into the trap of believing that all people are alike.

Paul's personalization of his ministry can be seen in the many lists of names included in his letters. He often praised individuals and communities and nearly always began correspondence with thanksgiving and intercessions for his audience (Rom. 1:8-13; 1 Cor. 1:4-8; Phil. 1:3-11; Col. 1:3-7; 1 Thess. 1:2-3). The fact that the subject matter of most of the epistles was dictated by the needs of the people assured audience interest. He preached about the problems the people brought to him. Paul preached to needs, those he perceived as universal such as sin, those that were community oriented such as eating meat offered to idols, and those that were personal such as instruction for Timothy and restoration for Onesimus. Paul did not, however, deal with individuals as often as Jesus did. Acts tells us of personal encounters, and the personal references in the Pauline literature imply that there were some, but they are not the highlight of Paul's ministry. Different personalities, different missions, different calls, and different cultures produce different forms. However, the preaching of Paul was focused more on people than propositions and was sensitive to needs and social environment.

Emotional Appeal

Paul appealed unashamedly to the emotions of his congregations. He wrote movingly of the love of God (1 Cor. 13; Rom. 8, 12; 1 Cor. 14:1, 16:24; 2 Cor. 8:7; Gal. 5:22; Eph. 3:17). He assured his audience that their well-being was his primary motivation; "it is all for your sake" (2 Cor. 4:15), he wrote, and "we work for your sake" (2 Cor. 1:24). "I want you to be free of anxieties," he wrote to the troubled Corinthians (1 Cor. 7:32). He did not hesitate to share his feelings about familial relationships in the spiritual community, "I became your father" (1 Cor. 4:15). In a particularly moving passage in the Second Letter to the Corinthians, he wrote of the relief from personal despair brought about by news of their response to his written rebuke of their conduct. He expressed joy resulting from "godly grief" that produced repentance in them (2 Cor. 7:5-16). He flattered individuals and groups when it was appropriate to the occasion (2 Cor. 9:2*ff.*; Rom. 1:8; Phil. 4:10-20). He expressed a special fondness for the Philippians, praising their past efforts and encouraging them to future service while at the same time relating his affection and longing for them (Phil. 1:3-10). Paul's evangelism was marked by the sincere appeal of a loving pastor.

Rational Appeal

Let us now turn to the content of Paul's preaching, his use of evidence and reasoning. He marshalled arguments to win intellectual assent to be combined with emotional stimulation that would evoke action from a self-conscious will. Paul often clearly stated a proposition to be proved. The proposition of Romans is stated in 1:16-17, "it [the gospel] is the power of God for salvation to everyone who has faith . . . in it the righteousness of God is revealed through faith for faith . . . ." The proposition of Galatians appears further in the text as the apostle makes the point that Jews and Gentiles alike are "not justified by works of the law but through faith in Jesus Christ" (Gal. 2:15-21). The longer manuscripts and confluent fragments of letters have subplots, units that can be treated as self-contained. Burton Mack identifies a number of these in *Rhetoric and the New Testament:*

> In fact Christ was raised from the dead, the first fruits of those who have died (1 Cor. 15:1-58, v. 20).
>
> Generous giving will be rewarded (2 Cor. 9, implied in v. 6).
>
> Agape is all that counts (1 Cor. 13, vv. 1-3).[4]

Paul frequently used the form of the syllogism to reason with his hearers. Most of the time he used the abbreviated form called by Aristotle an enthymeme. Scholars have written lengthy articles defining or describing the enthymeme but the simplest explanation is that it is a maxim which assumes a major or minor premise and infers a desired conclusion. 1 Corinthians 8:4 contains two in a discussion of eating food offered to idols. Paul declared that "an idol has no real existence," which easily leads to the conclusion that the non-existent cannot taint anything. "There is no God but one," he continued, with the clear implication that food cannot really be offered to any other divinity. Both of these statements were common beliefs of both Jews and Christians.

Paul argued from past "fact" to future possibility in the discussion of the resurrection in Chapter 15. He argued from the fact that Jesus has been raised from the dead to the hope of resurrection for believers. Even-handed divine justice for Jews and Greeks alike is predicated on the truth that "God shows no partiality" (Rom. 2:11). Paul's best known maxim is probably "all have sinned" (Rom. 3:23). "All" includes the listener who is guilty of sin and therefore in need of redemption. The key to this kind of argument is choosing a premise that fits the belief system of the audience. If they agree with the basic premise, they can be led to the desired conclusion. The flaw in such pulpit reasoning today is the choice of false or unshared premises. "The Bible says" may have no authority for those who have not read it, do not accept it as inspired literature, or treat it as fiction.

Paul's use of terse statements was perfect for an oral culture. It worked well from the perspective of hearing clearly and grasping meaning in short bits and also for the audience's memory. A few such pithy expressions follow:

Bad company ruins good morals (1 Cor. 15:33).

Let all that you do be done in love (1 Cor. 16:14).

The written code kills but the spirit gives life (2 Cor. 3:6).

If any one will not work, let him not eat (2 Thess. 3:10).

A little yeast leavens a whole loaf (1 Cor. 5:6).

Such statements as these become slogans that one remembers in the crucible of everyday life when encouragement or direction is needed. They are also easily shared with others and thus serve the dual purpose of making a point and being portable.

Paul's use of Scripture would (like Jesus') offend many contemporary exegetes. It is ironic that many preachers who rely heavily on Paul's writings and theology are so different in their treatment of sacred writings. Paul never employed the technique of delivering a running commentary on a text. Those who insist on a word-by-word or sentence-by-sentence explanation of the text find little support in the practice of Paul. His concept of expository preaching was an explanation and application of the truth of a text. When addressing believers he often used proof texts, a practice not encouraged today. This was a common practice of Stoics and rabbis in Paul's day, but presupposes accepted authority or the limited purpose of understanding, as opposed to transformation. Paul wanted his listeners to be moved to action as a result of his preaching.

Robin Scroggs's rhetorical treatment of Romans provides an excellent case study of Paul's use of scripture.[5] Scroggs argues that the main body of Romans is derived from two homilies preached for two different audiences. Romans 1—4 and 9—11, according to Scroggs, is sermonic material for a Jewish audience and chapters 5—8 constitute a sermon for a Greco-Roman audience. He points out that the message designed for the Jews is a well-developed argument that moves from creation to eschaton and heavily depends on Scripture using fifty-three citations. This sermon appeals to scriptural authority respected by the listeners. Paul did, however, radically reinterpret the meaning of Israelite history as reflected in the Scriptures. Scroggs calls the sermon in 5—8 a discourse on the Spirit and new life in Christ. This material includes only two explicit scriptural citations.

Paul adapted to the style and needs of his day as preachers must in every historical period and cultural context. Science as we know it and the inductive reasoning process did not dominate the thinking of persons in the first century as it does in the twentieth century. Paul would often quote a Scripture only as evidence and with no intention of explaining it. His discussion of the problem of "tongues"(1 Cor. 14:20*ff.*) includes a verse from Isaiah 28:11. The translation is not precisely from the extant Hebrew text or the Septuagint. He used this text to support his argument that speaking in tongues is a sign for unbelievers but really did not exegete the Isaiah passage, which seems to have nothing to do with his subject— ecstatic speech.[6] The rabbis, also, often took a broad general premise and applied it to a simple particular as Paul did when he reasoned that Christians can eat meat offered to idols because " 'the earth is the Lord's and all it contains' " (1 Cor. 10:25-26, NASB). In 1 Corinthians 9, Paul moved from a rational, common-sense argument to a proof text which he allegorized. He proceeded from the analogy of the missionary and a soldier entitled to upkeep to the right of a farmer to produce and a herdsman to milk. Then he used a text on animal protection from Deuteronomy 25:4 and applied it to the entitlement of apostles.[7] A text from historical narration in Exodus 16:18 is used in his appeal for the collection for Jerusalem as a commendation to share 2 Cor. 8:10-15). Paul's use of Scripture shows rabbinic influence in his tendency to combine isolated quotations from different sources,[8] for example, the tenth chapter of 1 Corinthians quotes or alludes to passages in Exodus, Numbers, Psalms, Leviticus, and Deuteronomy. Often Paul drew examples from the Scriptures. As one might expect a favorite is Abraham, the model of the true believer who lived by faith (Rom. 4:3; Gal. 3:6*ff.*).

Dynamic Analogy

Paul's use of narration and allegory demonstrated that he could appreciate the value of story in communicating the gospel. He often told his own conversion story and the accounts of his travels were reflections on how God had worked in his life. The clearest example of his use of allegory is found in Galatians 4:21-31 where he renders by his own description "an allegorical meaning" of the story of Hagar and Sarah. The preacher does not quote the scriptural account verbatim but tells the story. Paul used God's working with individuals in other periods as models for present and future. Another example of this method is found in the tenth chapter of 1 Corinthians where the liberation of Israel through the parting of the sea is called baptism and the rock that gave forth saving water is identified as the Christ (1 Cor. 10:1-5). Paul's allegory was more like what is known as typology. Past and present interact to shed meaning on separate events. Historical persons and events are viewed as objects, events, or persons—as "types" or figures of events to come. We understand later events from historical patterns. "The supernatural Rock which followed them," Paul said, "the Rock is Christ" (1 Cor. 10:4). The rock was not actually Christ but was a type of Christ in its power to give life. Hans Dieter Betz says that the Hagar passage is a mixture of allegory and typology. Typology has long been a more acceptable method to Christian exegetes. Betz contrasts the two:

Paul the Preacher

Typology interprets historical material commonly used in primitive Christianity. Persons, events, and institutions of scripture and tradition are taken as prototypes of present persons, events, and institutions, which are explained as their fulfillment, repetition, or completion within a framework of salvation history . . . allegory takes concrete matters mentioned in scripture and tradition . . . to be the surface appearance or vestige of underlying deeper truths which the method claims to bring to light. Thereby concrete matters in the text are transposed into general notions of philosophical or theological truths.[9]

Paul's technique might be characterized as dynamic analogy; Hagar personifies the covenant of law and slavery, Sarah the covenant of promise and freedom. This homiletical principle pulls together then and now, them and us. Those who would seduce believers through deception are like the serpent who led Eve astray (2 Cor. 11:3-4). False teachers who opposed Paul and Timothy were compared with the Egyptian magicians who opposed Moses (2 Tim. 3:1-9). The church is continually treated as the equivalent of Israel. Persons and situations in ancient cultures and places must be translated into persons and situations alike in essence but different in form in the preacher's time.

Forceful Argument

Much of Paul's preaching had a polemical cast to it. He presented ideas that challenged the status quo of both Jewish and Greek religions (and philosophic) thought. A major portion of his epistles was given to refuting charges against him and distortions of Christian teaching. A technique employed by Paul, especially in Romans, was the diatribe. George Kennedy, relying on Stanley K. Stowers, described the diatribe as a form of discourse in which a teacher "addresses and rebukes his students and refutes logical objections to his doctrines . . . ."[10] The preacher states opposing positions in the form of questions which are then answered. He anticipates questions or objections and answers them in such a way as to clarify his point and demonstrate the superiority of his conclusion. Excellent examples appear in Romans 3:1-8 and 3:9-

19. Scroggs identified the homily in Romans 5—8 as a model of a sermon in diatribe style. He responds to imagined interrogation in Romans 6:

> What shall we say then? Are we to continue in sin that grace may abound? By no means! How can we who died to sin still live in it? Do you not know that all of us who have been baptized into Christ Jesus were baptized into his death? We were buried therefore with him by baptism into death, so that as Christ was raised from the dead by the glory of the Father, we too might walk in newness of life.
> For if we have been united with him in a death like his, we shall certainly be united with him in a resurrection like his. We know that our old self was crucified with him so that the sinful body might be destroyed, and we might no longer be enslaved to sin. For he who has died is freed from sin. But if we have died with Christ, we believe that we shall also live with him. For we know that Christ being raised from the dead will never die again; death no longer has dominion over him. The death he died he died to sin, once for all, but the life he lives he lives to God. So you also must consider yourselves dead to sin and alive to God in Christ Jesus. (vv.1-11)

It is not difficult to answer questions that you ask yourself. Paul's questions were logical ones that may well have been in the mind of his correspondents. If the questions are not the questions the audience would ask, then the impact of answers will be negative.

Lively Illustrations

Paul's illustrations were drawn from life experience, nature, athletics, and the military. In Romans 11, he used a tree metaphor to discuss Israel's and the Gentile's relationship to God (cf. 2 Cor. 11:2). In Romans 7, he wrote that those married to the law have been set free by death and are married to Christ. The Hellenists loved their sports as much as modern Americans and would have understood Paul's metaphors drawn from gymnasium and stadium (1 Cor. 9:24-27; 2 Tim. 2:5, 4:7-8; Gal. 2:2, 5:7). There was appeal to the senses: taste (1 Cor. 3:1-3); kinetic (sleep, 1 Thess.

5:6); smell (2 Cor. 2:14-16); and sound (1 Cor. 14:6-8). Certainly a favorite metaphor for Paul, and one that transcends the ages, is that of the church as a body (1 Cor. 12; Col. 1:18, 2:10, 2:19; Eph. 4:4).

Comparison of the illustrations of Jesus and Paul reveals much about the effective use of illustration to clarify and to convince. Each preacher drew illustrations from personal experience and from common experience with the people who formed an immediate audience. They did not use the same illustrations except in such universal experiences as eating and sleeping. Most of those who heard Jesus were Jews living in the homeland. They shared a common history, common religious tradition, and lived in a homogeneous culture—primarily in small towns, villages, and the countryside. They were farmers, fishers, professional religious, and craftspersons. Those who heard Paul, on the other hand, were diaspora Jews and Greco-Romans, people of the world who spoke different languages, were exposed to different philosophies, emerged from different ethnic and religious traditions, and were heterogeneous. Even the Jews Paul addressed had different lifestyles and points of reference from the Jews who were Jesus' audience. "The Judaism of the dispersion . . . had its own peculiar character, now scoffed at and now respected by other Jews, shunned by some and aspired to by others, notorious for its strange customs, famous for its faith in God and the purity of its morals."[11] As is often the case with people living as aliens, the Jews of the dispersion may have been more restrictive in their religious practices and beliefs because of a fear of synchretism.

The non-Jews whom Paul encountered were diverse, secular, and metropolitan in viewpoint. Paul's audience on his travels included "government officials, traders, pilgrims, the sick, letter carriers, sightseers, runaway slaves, fugitives, prisoners, athletes, artisans, teachers and students."[12] Jesus and Paul worked on the principle of communicating the unfamiliar by analogy (literal and figurative) with the familiar. The nature of their specific illustrations differed because their audiences were different. The same conclusion may be drawn about their reasoning and sources of authority.

Logical Organization

Paul's conscious arrangement of his thoughts followed the classical pattern of dialogue. Kennedy states that this was true of Paul's letters, which were not unique in this respect. "The structure of a Greco-Roman letter," Kennedy observes, resembles a speech, "framed by a salutation and complimentary closure."[13] I have pointed out above that Paul's salutations and closures were intentioned with ethical and emotional appeal. The standard form of a speech included an introduction, statement of the case, supporting arguments, and conclusions. The introduction sought to establish interest in the subject and to win approval or trust for the speaker. The statement of the case focused on the nature of the speech, its purpose, and the proposition or issue. Arguments included refutation of real or imaginary opposition and the speaker's evidence and explanation. The conclusion might be weighted to an intellectual or emotional appeal for a favorable judgment (in the case of judicial speeches) or an appeal for specific action (in deliberative speeches). Burton Mack includes in his examination of Paul's rhetoric outlines of some short units that illustrate Paul's organization. One such outline is the following stewardship homily in 2 Corinthians 9:1-15:

An Exhortation to Contribute

Exordium: Address to the audience with praise for their earlier promise and readiness to contribute. (vv. 1-2)

Narration: Paul sends the letter and the brothers in advance to make sure that when he arrives with the Macedonians, he will not be humiliated and the Achaians will not be forced by shame into keeping a promise as yet unfulfilled. (vv. 3-5)

Thesis: Generous giving will be rewarded. (implied, v. 6)

The Argument: (vv. 6-10)

Analogy: Sowing and reaping. (v. 6)

Proverb: God loves a cheerful giver. (LXX Prov. 22:8; v. 7)

Pronouncement: God is able to provide in abundance. (v. 8)

Citation: "God scatters, gives to the poor; his righteousness endures." (Ps. 119:9; v.9)

Conclusion: God will supply the seed, multiply the sowing, and increase the harvest, both of physical resources and of your righteousness. (vv. 10-11a)

The Exhortation: (vv. 11-14)

Honor: The challenge is a test of faith and obedience to the gospel.

Virtue: Passing the test will demonstrate the virtues of faith, obedience, generosity, piety, and grace.

Reward: Others will recognize your Christian virtue, pray for you, and give thanks to God.

Conclusion: Thanks be to God. (v. 15)[14]

Paul's strategy was to lead his audience through a process of thought and bring them to the desired conclusion and action. Belief (thought) was to produce action. He usually showed them the personal benefits that would derive from choosing the particular course of action he prescribed. He urged the Colossians to serve the Lord and "receive the inheritance as your reward . . . for the wrongdoer will be paid back for the wrong . . . done" (Col. 3:24-25). He exhorted the Thessalonians to love and work "so that you may command the respect of outsiders and be dependent on nobody" (1 Thess. 4:12). He further told them to "keep awake and be sober" (1 Thess. 5:6) in order to obtain "salvation through our Lord Jesus Christ" (5:9). Focus on the noble and obey what they've been taught, he wrote the Philippians and "the God of peace will be with you" (Phil. 4:9). His discourse on the resurrection in 1 Corinthians 15 offers the resurrection hope to those who are "steadfast, immovable, always abounding in the work of the Lord" (15:58). Paul arranged his arguments to present a problem and then offer an attractive solution to the listeners. He often contrasted these benefits to the negative consequences which would result from following their present course.

Scroggs's analysis of the theological material in Romans 1—11 demonstrates that Paul varied arrangement according to audience and purpose as he adapted other elements of rhetoric. The sermon to the Jews in 1—4 and 9—11 is a tightly developed argument while the sermon to the Gentiles is circular with a refrain of the central theme—victory of God over death through Christ. Paul used the rhetorical device of the "mystic ladder" for the more philosophical Gentiles.[15] This chain was a device popular in Hellenistic literature. Scroggs cites 5:3-5 as an example of this technique:

> More than that, we rejoice in our sufferings, knowing that suffering produces endurance, and endurance produces character, and character produces hope, and hope does not disappoint us, because God's love has been poured into our hearts through the Holy spirit which has been given to us. (cf. 8:29)

Paul also employed the technique of using the introduction and conclusion as bookends. Themes clearly stated in the beginning and the end hold the segments together. Glory, hope, suffering, Spirit, and agape are introduced in 5:2-5 and developed into the climax in 8:12-39.[16]

Vigorous Style

Paul's style is vigorous and vivid. The oral character of his prose is quickly evident when it is read aloud. His sentences are short and usually simple. The maxims or proverbs that are interspersed throughout his correspondence state truth simply, clearly, and memorably. "Let no one seek his own good, but the good of his neighbor" (1 Cor. 10:24). "Do not be deceived; God is not mocked, for whatever a man sows, that he will also reap" (Gal. 6:7). "We know that in everything God works for good with those who love him, who are called according to his purpose" (Rom. 8:28). These pithy statements were easy to grasp when they were heard. They appealed to the ear in their terseness and the thought was clear. Remember that most people would hear rather than see Paul's rhetoric. The letters were read in public gatherings. Contemporary preachers should write their sermons to the ear rather

than to the eye. Paul's use of questions was not limited to the dia-
tribes. Questions that call for mental involvement on the part of
the reader-hearer liberally appear in his texts. Questions focus
thought and are the most common means of involving listeners in
mental conversation, thus making them active listeners.

Paul showed a decided preference for the active indicative voice.
He rarely used the passive voice. He used verbs that described or
called for action. He spoke with authority as to what was and will
be. Examine the verbs in Galatians 6:1-9 and consider their
strength: *live, walk, have, restore, look, bear, thinks, deceives, test,
will have to bear, taught, share, deceived, mocked, sows, reap, grow,
do.* The variety and vigor are remarkable. His choice of words and
sentence structure have a dynamic rhythm. First Corinthians
13:4-7 is a remarkable example of strong verbs and moving
cadence.

> Love is patient and kind; love is not jealous or boastful; it is not
> arrogant or rude. Love does not insist on its own way; it is not
> irritable or resentful; it does not rejoice at wrong, but rejoices in the
> right. Love bears all things, believes all things, hopes all things,
> endures all things.

Style is concerned with the choice of words and their composition. Preachers often get carried away with adjectives, but verbs
control the power of speech. Paul exercised great economy in his
use of adjectives and great strength in his selection of verbs.

Paul chose language that had emotional appeal. Words like *love,
humble, yearn, affection,* and *joy* were prominent in his vocabulary. He spoke often with great tenderness such as when he wrote
the Thessalonians that he was "gentle . . . like a nurse taking care
of her children" (1 Thess. 2:7). He was an artist with aural images
that said much with few words as when he wrote "admonish the
idlers, encourage the fainthearted, help the weak, be patient with
them all" (1 Thess. 5:14). Words like *grumbling, questioning,
blameless,* and *innocent* had an everyday texture and instant image
recognition. Paul used language that soothed and was winsome,
but he also used it to sting and mock. The sudden shift in tone in

Philippians 3:2 has led many to conclude that it is a fragment of another letter inserted in the manuscript. Words of affection are replaced by words of warning against "dogs," "evil workers," "those who mutilate the flesh." He warned the Colossians to resist those "puffed up without reason by his sensuous mind" (2:18). He contrasted Christian qualities with those of the old life, "anger, wrath, malice, slander and foul talk" (3:8). The language he used combined sound with meaning for impact. Consider the sounds of selected phrases: "noisy gong," "clanging cymbal" (1 Cor. 13:1), "puffs up" versus "builds up" (1 Cor. 8:1), the "sword of the Spirit" (Eph. 6:17); "grumbling or questioning" (Phil. 2:14), "stable and steadfast" (Col. 1:23). A preacher should choose language for its total impact and that includes sound and feeling as much as meaning. Preachers do well to read their sermons aloud as they construct them. The oral quality of Paul's epistles may be due in part to the fact that he dictated them. Paul's use of an extensive vocabulary drawn from human experience and literary sources left little doubt about his feelings, what he loved and what he hated.

Conclusion

Paul's writings make clear that he arranged and expressed thought purposefully. He strategized with message and audience in mind. He presented himself in such a way as to establish credibility. He exposed his vulnerabilities in order to identify with his audience. He took the risk of disclosing his weaknesses to prove that he understood theirs. He did not assume or demand respect, he earned it. He demonstrated knowledge, integrity, and genuine care for whatever group he was addressing. He chose his authoritative sources, evidence, illustrations, and language intentionally. He particularized his message for specific situations, problems, and people. He worked at removing cultural stumbling blocks so that the message could be clearly and attractively presented. Paul made it a point to know his audience, appeal to their interests, and address their needs. His powerful intellect, broad experience, and training were applied to the form of the message as well as the message itself. Paul seemed to understand long before the development of contemporary communication theory that medium and message cannot be separated.

Notes

1. Martin Dibelius, *Studies in the Acts of the Apostles,* ed. Henrich Greven (London: SCM Press Ltd., 1956), 156.
2. See Hans Dieter Betz, *Galatians* (Philadelphia: Fortress Press, 1979), 74-75.
3. Plato, "Phaedus," *The Works of Plato,* trans. Benjamin Jowett, ed. Irwin Edman (New York: The Modern Library, 1956), 316*ff.*
4. Mack, 56, 59, 65.
5. Robin Scroggs, "Paul as Rhetorician: Two Homilies in Romans 1—11," *Jews, Greeks and Christians: Religious Cultures in Late Antiquity,* ed. Robert Homerton-Kelly and Robin Scroggs (Leiden: E. J. Brill, 1976), 271-98.
6. Dibelius, *Paul,* 39*ff.*
7. Hans Conzelmann, *1 Corinthians* (Philadelphia: Fortress Press, 1975), 241-42.
8. Ibid., 151*ff.*
9. Dieter Betz, 239.
10. Kennedy, 155.
11. Dibelius, *Paul,* 15.
12. Ronald Hock, quoted in Meeks, 16.
13. Kennedy, 141.
14. Mack, 59-60. He includes in the book a lengthy outline of the book of Galatians (69-70). A serious student of this topic will find it interesting to compare and contrast Mack's analysis with that of George Kennedy (142-44) and that of Hans Dieter Betz (16-23). Kennedy and Dieter Betz both offer a rhetorical analysis but differ on their opinion of the type of rhetoric the book represents. Kennedy contends that Galatians is deliberative and Dieter Betz that it is judicial. Betz sees Paul's intention to defend his presentation of the gospel, and Kennedy interprets the purpose to persuade the Galatians to continue in the Christian faith uncorrupted by legalistic Judaism. It is interesting to note that in an earlier work, Kennedy classified Galatians as "apology" (*Classical Rhetoric and Its Christian and Secular Tradition,* 130).
15. Scroggs, 285.
16. Ibid.

6

Paul's Sermons in Acts

There are nine speeches attributed to Paul in the book of Acts.[1] The speeches were delivered before Jews, Christians, and Gentiles. Paul spoke to high officials and ordinary citizens, rich and poor, educated and ignorant. Some of the sermons were delivered in synagogues, others in public forums, and others in trial contexts before government officials. One was delivered to shipwreck survivors on an island; one in the house where the preacher was under arrest. These speeches present us variations on a theme. Paul's message was essentially the same, but the forms of the messages were adapted to particular listeners. The good news of Jesus Christ is presented in different forms to different audiences.

These self-contained units of various lengths provide paradigms easily applied to the preaching situation. Three speeches with three different purposes delivered to three distinct audiences provide diverse applications of Paul's homiletical principles. The first recorded missionary sermon delivered in the synagogue in Antioch of Pisidia will be the first analyzed. Next comes Paul's first sermon to a Gentile audience, followed by a farewell sermon to the leaders of the church at Ephesus. The audiences represent distinctive groups in distinctive settings and at different levels in their understanding of God. One was Jewish with a common belief base as regards God, one was pagan, and the third was Christian.

Good News for Jews

The speech at Antioch of Pisidia (13:16-41) occurred in the context of synagogue worship. These were primarily services of the word. There would have been several prayers, scripture reading, and exhortation. Paul was unknown to the audience, and there was no evidence of overt hostility or favor. As a Jewish male adult,

Paul had the right to speak. The text suggests a dramatic moment as this stranger raised his hand for silence and began a familiar recitation of the history of Israel. He subtly laid the foundation for his anticipated conclusion by affirming their professed faith. The basic premise of his argument was that they "fear God." He went on to relate that their reverence for God was rooted in their ethnic experience of God's covenant with them. The first point of the sermon was that "God chose our fathers." The inference was that they were chosen and had historically received special treatment and revelation. Paul supported this point by citing the deliverance from Egyptian bondage, the wilderness, God's power in the conquest of Palestine, and the gift of the land. He then reminded them of the judges and the monarchy. He spoke of David whom God called "a man after my heart" and the prototype for the Messiah. A congregation so disposed might well have been rendering a chorus of *amens* to this point; at least there would have been heads nodding in agreement. It was a proud heritage.

Paul identified with them by citing common heritage and demonstrating that he was knowledgeable about their history. Here, as in Romans 1—4, 9—11, Paul reinterpreted the meaning of Israel's history. He built on a common field of experience and accepted authority. He also established the premise that God had given them special revelation in the past and had directly intervened in their lives. If they accepted this premise, as most of them likely did, then a strong argument could be made that God had given a new revelation and intervened more recently. Paul shrewdly laid the foundation for the new belief he wanted them to accept.

At this point Paul made a transition to Jesus. He moved from the accepted belief and undisputed data to the new revelation that he wanted them to believe. He did not attack their belief but sought to build on it. The second point, the proposition of the sermon, was that Jesus was the promised Savior. He used John's testimony to support his thesis. John, however, did not have prophetic status with all Israelites and while his ministry may have been known to the audience, it certainly did not have the authority of the prophets whose writings and history were a part of Hebrew sacred literature and tradition. Note, however, that Paul presented it matter-of-factly, without apology or explanation, as reliable testimony. His handling of the materials was as important as the material; he attributed authority to John's witness. Of course, Paul had accepted the authority of John's witness and spoke with personal conviction.

Paul then resorted to pathetic appeal, the special status of his listeners. He returned to his theme of "the chosen." Strong emotional appeal was contained in their identity as children of Abraham and their devotion to God (he repeated his appeal to those who "fear God"). He stressed identification as he shifted from "you" to "us" (v. 26). They were special, he told them, and therefore God had sent them the special word of salvation. The implication was that they would understand and accept Christian revelation because of their national experience.

What followed was an implied warning and a promised reward. They should not make the mistake of "those who live in Jerusalem and their rulers" (v. 27) and reject the one sent by God. He presented the *kerygma*, the death and resurrection of Jesus.[2] One advantage Paul had in this situation over the one in Athens was that all of his audience had heard discussions of a resurrection. It was not a new, shocking idea that people could be resurrected. Those influenced by the Pharisees would have believed in the possibility. He began in this section with a strong appeal to Scripture and tradition, authorities accepted by this audience. It is important to know what the audience already believes and what they will accept as authoritative.

Proof is not what the speaker accepts, but what will convince the audience. Proof always resides in the mind of the listener in a persuasive situation. Proof should not be confused with truth. The fact that someone believes and speaks the truth does not guarantee that it will be accepted. On the other hand, people often believe lies. The preacher must ask what will transmit the truth. Paul's indictment of the actions of those who had condemned Jesus was based on the fact "they did not recognize him nor understand the utterances of the prophets which are read every sabbath" (v. 27).

He asserted Jesus' innocence and the fact that Jesus was not convicted of any crime. Scripture was cited as predicting the events, and the events were a fulfillment of Scripture. What occurred "fulfilled all that was written of him" (v. 29). Paul did not begin with Scripture but used it to support his crucial point. He added to his scriptural support the evidence of eyewitnesses to the resurrection. He told them, in essence, that the new sect was led by people who saw these things happen. Paul stressed continuity with the faith of their common ancestors. He gave no impression that he was introducing a new religion, only a new revelation.

Paul moved from the agreed upon to a new idea which he argued was consistent with what was already believed. He then turned to its meaning for his hearers. This was the critical *so what?* of his sermon. Preachers sometimes share history and prophecy without applying it specifically to their audience. There needs to be a *so what?* statement that discloses what it means to the audience and what concrete effect it will have on them. This was "good news" (v. 32) he declared to them and that "through this man forgiveness of sins is proclaimed to you" (v. 38). He presented the consequences of receiving the message, forgiveness of sins and freedom, and the consequences of not receiving the message, "Behold you scoffers, and wonder, and perish." The judgment uttered on unbelief came directly from Scripture. His major points were based on direct appeal to Scripture, the authority of which was affirmed by the congregation. Indeed, he spoke at a time in the worship service when interpretation of Scripture and exhortation based on Scripture was expected.

This speech called for conviction and belief rather than specific action.[3] Paul planned to continue his dialogue with this congregation. He did not approach this as a one-time opportunity and try to do everything in a single presentation. He laid a foundation for further revelation and instruction. This presentation, like many of those recorded in Acts, reads like one part of an on-going conversation. Preachers often try to pack too much into a single sermon and overwhelm the audience so that nothing is really comprehended. Most of Paul's sermons recorded in Acts have only one point.

Even the Epistles usually have one central theme with several applications. I have heard preachers try to cover six or seven points in a sermon, and this in a culture conditioned for short television "bites" and unaccustomed to long lectures or extended periods of concentration of any kind. An audience is entitled to one clear idea in every message but that may be enough.

Paul left them wanting to hear more. "As they went out, the people begged that these things might be told them the next sabbath" (v. 42). Paul was willing to lead people a step at a time. This tactic required patience and perseverance on his part. Better that they should clamor for more than complain of too much. "The next sabbath almost the whole city gathered together to hear the word of God" (v. 44).

Aristotle said that the ideal pattern for advocacy would be to state a case and prove it. This seems to be exactly what Paul did at Antioch of Pisidia. There was no introduction or conclusion. The apostle stated his case and then offered support for it. Arrangement moved from the known to the unknown, from that which was already believed to new belief. He used language and images familiar and emotionally strong. Some of the sentences are longer than the average in the epistles but none of them are exceedingly long and involved. Short sentences are so interspersed as to keep a sense of movement and action.

Good News for Gentiles

Acts 17:16-34 is a passage popularly known as the Mars Hill sermon or the Areopagus Speech.[4] It is undoubtedly the most discussed and debated speech in the Bible (with the possible exception of the Sermon on the Mount). This is a model evangelistic sermon. The event takes place in a public forum with no indication that there were any Jews or God-fearers present. This was a marketplace presentation of the gospel to Gentiles. The main point and climax of this sermon is the same as at Antioch of Pisidia, but Paul arrived at his proclamation of the resurrection via a quite different route. A comparison of these two events demonstrates how Paul adapted to audience and cultural context.

Paul the Preacher

Paul did not limit his service; he argued with Jews, devout persons, and philosophers (vv. 17-18), in the synagogue and in the marketplace. He did not insist on the security of a controlled environment and a stacked audience. Two specific schools of philosophy are mentioned: Epicurean and Stoic. Paul seemed to be as familiar with these pagan philosophies as he was with his Jewish heritage. Missionaries have long understood that they must be well versed in the religions and cultures of the people to whom they preach. No matter where one preaches, effective preaching requires an understanding of the values and belief systems of the audience. Preachers must demonstrate knowledge to win respect and trust (ethical persuasion), and they must teach from known to unknown and understand what is accepted as authority (logical persuasion). Paul was well prepared. One does not have to go to a foreign field to be involved in a cross-cultural communication situation. A preacher reared in a rural culture who preaches in an urban setting must study the culture; that is, language, occupations, family patterns, the whole range of life experience. There are many subcultures in the United States and what works with a white Anglo-Saxon group may not be effective with blacks, hispanics, or Eastern Europeans. Arguments that convince blue-collar audiences may fail with college groups. One must know and appeal to specific audiences to be effective.

The Stoics and the Epicureans might well represent different branches of modern secular humanism. Observing how Paul addressed them may provide some workable strategies for dealing with modern skeptics and scholars. Both Stoics and Epicureans believed that they had found a way to live meaningful lives without God or hope beyond earthly existence. The Stoics urged people to seek rational existence without feeling. Virtue was its own reward. Everyone should conform to nature and devote themselves to meaningful work. Apathy characterized their attitude toward hopes for a better world.

Stoics had high ethical standards and contributed many good things to their communities. They believed that personal satisfaction derived from service. They had great respect for the natural order. These values provided a solid basis for hearing about the God of creation and the ethics of social responsibility inferred in Christian doctrine.

The Epicureans have been portrayed by many modern preachers as a-moralists who lived by the slogan, "eat, drink and be merry for tomorrow we die." Many interpret this as an invitation to debauchery and sexual immorality. The truth is that the Epicureans were responsible citizens and patrons of the fine arts. Many a contemporary philanthropist applauded by the world conforms to their life-style. They did believe that the end of life is happiness, and the pursuit of pleasure is the means to that end. They taught that the nobler things of life—education, art, beauty and public service—produced pleasure. They were also the cultured despisers of religion in their time. Like many of today's sophisticates they believed that religion was the enemy of progress and the province of ignorance and fear. Respect for beauty and a strong sense of public duty provided common ground for dialogue with Christianity.

Karl Barth is purported to have said that religion is the greatest obstacle to Christianity. That seems to have been the case in Athens. Superstition abounded there and Paul pointed out that they were "very religious" or "too superstitious" (KJV). They were people who wanted to know the truth and to understand the supernatural. Paul saw this as an opening through which he could carry the gospel. We do well to remember that one of the charges brought against Christians in pagan cultures was that they were atheists because they did not believe in all the gods. The jealousness of the Christian God and the exclusivity of the faith were obstacles with which early Christian teachers and preachers had to contend. There are many today who operate out of a cultural relativism that teaches that one religion is as good as another and "it doesn't matter what you believe as long as you believe something."

Paul began this sermon at some disadvantage. The audience was not neutral in their attitude toward him. His arguments in the marketplace had earned him a reputation as a "babbler" (v. 18) and preacher of "foreign divinities." It appears that he was invited to speak out of curiosity, a diversion from their ordinary dialogue and debate. Paul was not the first or the last preacher to be heard out of curiosity, nor would he be the last. He had to overcome negative perceptions to hope for any real hearing. Of course in this day of television evangelists and bizarre performances labeled preaching events, not to mention exposés of moral turpitude on the part of Christian ministers, there are negative perceptions to be overcome to get a hearing of the gospel. Some scholars argue that Paul was brought before the council to defend his teachings because those who had heard him thought his foolish teachings were a threat to the intellectual integrity of the city and wanted to silence him. In either case Paul carried with him no personal authority.

Paul did not begin with a defense of himself or an open attack on his audience. What he did seek was identification. He focused on common interests and goals. He began where his audience was intellectually and culturally. He strove to take them from the known to the unknown and to lead them to the next stage of revelation. He seems to have assured them that through general or natural revelation they had some intuitive awareness of the true God. This is consistent with the theology he enunciated in Romans 1:18—3:20. Paul proceeded to show respect for their heritage by quoting from familiar writings. He began where *they* were rather than where he was. He did not begin by quoting the Bible or appealing to biblical authority. Using the Bible as a source of overt authority to those unfamiliar with it is senseless. The Scriptures are self-authenticating but should be introduced in narrative form rather than as legal documents. The Bible can be used as an interpreter of human experience. Remember, the focus must be on what the congregation accepts as proof. He did present the message of the Bible and was true to the revelation to which the Scriptures bear witness. He sought to lead them to new discoveries but by first taking them over familiar ground.

Paul's theological strategy is interesting and one worth serious consideration in dealing with Christian or non-Christian audiences. He did not begin with humanity but with God and creation. Some take offense at any notice of "natural theology" but Paul seemed to have rooted his argument in the revelation of God in the natural order and universal human experience (Romans 1:18— 3:20). Bertil Gartner has persuasively argued that the doctrine of natural revelation was a part of early missionary preaching. "The reference to creation and its attenuation of God was probably an integral part of the oldest Christian missionary preaching: here the Gentile and the Christian could meet on common ground and human experiences would be used in illustration."[5] It was the "unknown" true God that Paul was identifying. He told them in effect that they instinctively reached out for this God, but could not name Him and did not know how to relate to Him. God is the one whose hand is revealed in nature and history. Paul appealed to reason and experience as the foundation for his proclamation of the special redemptive revelation in Jesus Christ. Paul found in other religions basis for conversation leading to disclosure of resurrection faith. Contemporary preachers need to understand the beliefs and cults with which they are contending if they expect to be effective.

From a discussion of the cosmos, the preacher moved to humans and their role in the created world. An important distinction made between Stoic-Epicurean thought and Christian thought is that the latter teaches that God is acting to preserve the world. He is not a mere cause who sets the natural order in operation and withdraws. He is the ruler who providentially oversees history and persons. The Stoics believed the world was controlled by rational necessity, and the Epicureans thought history was purposeless, governed by accidents. This was knowledge important to a speaker who wanted to reshape their thought. Again Paul asserted that God was revealing Himself to persons in ways other than Judaeo-Christian tradition. He implied that there is an innate urge in human hearts to "seek God, in the hope that they might feel after him and find him." Augustine, the early church father, gave a personal testimony to such promptings in *Confessions* where he wrote: "Thou madest us for Thyself, and our heart is restless until it repose in thee."[6] We might paraphrase as follows: All persons are made for God and will not find peace until they are reconciled to Him. The Christian evangelist may appeal to the often nameless (unknown) longing of human hearts for purpose and meaning.

Paul appealed to their intellect with regard to idolatry. He implied that their concept of God was greater than that which could be conceived in a work of art created by human agency. Their thought, he suggested, was beyond primitive notions of human-made gods who lacked even human abilities. Paul used a classical syllogism in his discussion of God (vv. 24-25).

God made the world
He needs nothing
Therefore service to idols is useless

His basic premise was implicit in the religion of the Stoics and the Epicureans's sense of natural order. He moved toward his evangelistic purpose with an enthymeme on God's relationship to humanity (vv. 26-27).

God made all humanity
He made them to seek Him
(implied) You are human, created to seek Him.

This form of argument was common in philosophical debate and the point would have been easily grasped by this audience.

"The times of ignorance" (v. 30) and natural theology anticipated the Roman correspondence of later years (1:18-23) with the judgment that all are without excuse. The evangelist charged his listeners to act upon that which they knew and to move toward that to which their natural inclination, experience, and knowledge led them.

The sermon reached a climax in verses 30-31 with the pronouncement of the resurrection, impending judgment, and the call to repentance. "Now" things are different, more is demanded. He stated the reality of the resurrection as fact, knowing full well that there was no "natural theology" evidence to support his report.

He used reason and experience as far as it would take him but then moved beyond that to the scandal of the cross. Paul fashioned his call for repentance to fit the situation. All persons need to repent but not always from the same misunderstandings, deficient knowledge, or behavior.

> Repentance for the Jew means turning away from the rejection of Jesus and toward the Messiah Jesus. Repentance for the Stoic, however, means turning away from his understanding of God as the built-in law of the universe (actually his ignorance of God) to worship the God who transcends creation. In other words, in this sermon on Mars Hall, Paul recognizes that each person must make his own repentance in his own way, in light of the situation in which the gospel finds him.[7]

Remember Paul's own conversion was not from a life of licentiousness but from a misunderstanding of God's working. He was called from dependence on the law to acceptance of grace, and he invited the philosophers to turn from human reason to the wisdom of God revealed in Christ.

Paul appealed to the Greek philosophers in their own language. He drew upon their tradition and literature as he had appealed to the different tradition and literature of the Jews at Antioch in Pisidia. He showed great respect for them and their tradition and tried to win their respect by demonstrating his knowledge of their thought and literature. He identified himself and his faith with their goals. He used rhetorical techniques in a setting where they would be respected and effective.

Once again this sermon does not have an introduction because Paul was invited to present his theology. Interest was established and any direct appeal for acceptance was doomed. He was interrupted before he could formally conclude with a direct appeal. J. Estill Jones pulled the following outline from the sermon:

1. You know many gods (vv. 22-23)
2. I present to you *the* God (vv. 24-29)
(1) He is creator of all things (vv. 24-25)
(2) He is sovereign and sufficient (v. 26)

(3) He made men
all men, that they should seek him and find him, for he is near
(vv. 27-28)
(4) He is Spirit (v. 29)
3. You are to repent (vv. 30-31)
(1) God commands it (v. 30)
(2) God will judge the world (v. 31)
in righteousness by a man whom he raised from the dead (v.
31).[8]

Some have called this sermon a failure because of the response
of ridicule and because there were not many conversions. Because
Paul went from Athens to Corinth some scholars view Paul's cri-
tique of worldly wisdom in 1 Corinthians 1—2 as a repudiation of
his methodology in Athens. Was the sermon a failure? I don't
think so and I don't think Paul thought so. "Some mocked," but
"others said, 'We will hear you again.'" Does it not often take
more than one encounter, more than one presentation of the gospel to effect a conversion? Rarely are persons converted today on
the first hearing of the gospel in a twenty-five-minute sermon.
There were some immediate conversions from an audience un-
schooled in Old Testament and not conditioned in an environment
of monotheism. This is the wonder of the occasion that *any* immediately converted. The gospel was preached, heard, and received
by some. Remember the responsibility of those who listen. Paul
did everything that was in his power to create a climate in which
the Word within could work with the Word proclaimed. Paul
trusted the Spirit and the Word.

This was neither the first nor the last time the preaching of the
gospel provoked mockery, rejection, even violence. Luke recorded
many such instances and history is replete with them. Did not
Paul initially react violently to the gospel? His first response to
Christian teaching had been that it was worse than fantasy, it was
an attack on truth. Perhaps some of the skeptics at Athens became
preachers and teachers of the faith as Paul had. We sometimes
expect too much of one encounter and surrender too easily.

As to Paul's methodology in Acts 17:16*ff.*, he did not abandon it. The Epistle to the Romans begins with a commentary on natural theology and 1 Corinthians 15:33 records a quotation from Epicurean philosophy. His message was always adapted to particular audiences. I am inclined to agree with Hans Conzelmann's assessment that this passage "is the most momentous Christian document from the beginnings of that extraordinary confrontation between Christianity and philosophy."[9] It provides, moreover, a splendid model for similar encounters with cultured despisers of religion. It is a model that has been used many times through the centuries. What we have in Acts 17:16-34 is a stunning example of what it means to "become all things to all men, that I might by all means save some" (1 Cor. 9:22).

Good News for Believers

The speech to the elders from Ephesus at Miletus (20:17-37) has special significance because it is the one speech in Acts that is directed to the Christian community and it is the last public speech before Paul's imprisonment.[10] It is a highly personal speech with strong ethos and pathos. He reminded them of his service and suffering among them and on their behalf. He told them that the Spirit had revealed that the journey upon which he was embarking would bring him great suffering.

Emotional appeal was strong as he related personal sacrifice and the "blood" of Christ to the mission. He lovingly recalled their efforts on his behalf and affirmed their roles of leadership. He blessed them and commended them to God. This speech is primarily epideictic in its praise of their mutual dedication and work. He focused on the future only in calling for continued faithfulness. He presented no new doctrine and called for no behavioral change. He confirmed their belief and encouraged the faith they already possessed.

Paul employed a powerful metaphor of the wolf attacking the flock. The main thought was that the elders had been entrusted with the work. The Holy Spirit had called them "to care for the church of God" (v. 28). Strong argument or evidence was not required where common belief and commitment existed. Preachers

Paul the Preacher

often tell me that Easter and Christmas present them with the greatest difficulties in sermon preparation because there is nothing new to be said. Every preaching situation does not require some new idea or assignment. Encouragement and confirmation are important elements in deepening faith and keeping people on mission.

Preaching events often include more than words spoken. The climax of the Miletus episode was the rhetorical action described in 20:36-37:

> And when he had spoken thus, he knelt down and prayed with them all. And they all wept and embraced Paul and kissed him, sorrowing most of all because of the word he had spoken, that they should see his face no more. And they brought him to the ship.

"He knelt down," an act of humility, and "prayed with them," an act of faith and identity. All wept, embraced, and kissed—powerful emotional acts. These acts would remain as motivating memories long after words had been forgotten. They would be moved to hard work and sustained in difficult circumstances by these sensory memories. Preachers should think of worship as proclamation events. Embraces and handshakes are ethical appeals. Acts of kneeling, receiving the ordinances, and the raised hand of blessing contribute to the impact of a rhetorical event. Acted parables such as the Lord's Supper and baptism are a part of our proclamation. Every public act before, during, and after a sermon will have an impact on the reception of the message. Proclamation is an event, and the preacher should be sensitive to the impressions of the physical and visual as well as the intellectual and aural.

Conclusion

These three examples of Paul's oratory exhibit his use of the rhetorical principles previously discussed. He was aware of attitudes toward him and sought to favorably dispose the audience to him through identification and displayed knowledge. He spoke with authority. He demonstrated knowledge of the people to whom he spoke and appealed to their emotions. He used reason

Paul's Sermons in Acts

and evidence in an ordered manner. His arrangement was designed to lead the audience step by step toward his goal. Language was forceful and composition was dynamic. His sermons, while brief, are good paradigms for the contemporary proclaimer. It might be noted that he was able to pack a great deal into a small time and space. Even his brevity might be worth emulating.

Notes

1. Acts 13:16-41; 14:15-17; 17:22-31; 20:18-35; 22:1-21; 24:10-21; 26:2-23,25-27; 27:21-26; 28:17-20. I am aware of the continuing debate as to the reliability of Acts for Paul's biography and the authenticity of the speeches of Paul. Did Luke construct these speeches himself? Did he edit and fashion them from notes from Paul's sermons to create an ideal sermon form for the early church? Did Paul preach them exactly as we have them? For our purpose, it really does not matter. The church has accepted and canonized them. They are models undoubtedly representing what was considered the best of first-century preaching.

2. See C. H. Dodd's discussion of the fundamental message of the apostles, indeed the true preaching of the early church in *The Apostolic Preaching and Its Development* (Grand Rapids: Baker Book House, reprint 1980). He discusses Pauline *kerygma* on 13*ff.* He summarizes from his various Pauline sources Paul's message as follows:

The prophecies are fulfilled, and the new Age is inaugurated by the coming of Christ.

He was born of the seed of David.

He died according to the Scriptures, to deliver us out of the present evil age.

He was buried.

He rose on the third day according to the Scriptures.

He is exalted at the right hand of God, as Son of God and Lord of quick and dead.

He will come again as Judge and Saviour of men. (17).

3. Kennedy, 124-25.

4. Much of the material in this section was previously published in an expository article in *The Review and Expositor.*

5. Bertil Gartner, *The Areopagus Speech and Natural Revelation* (Uppsala: C. Wik. Gleerup, 1955), 176*ff.*

6. Augustine, *The Confessions*, Great Books of the Western World, ed. Robert Maynard Hutchins, 5.18.1.

Paul the Preacher

7. Leander E. Keck, *Mandate to Witness* (Valley Forge: Judson Press, 1964), 121-22.

8. J. Estill Jones, *Acts: Working Together in Christ's Mission* (Nashville: Convention Press, 1974), 101-2.

9. Hans Conzelmann, "The Address of Paul on the Areopagus." *Studies in Luke-Acts*, ed. Leander Keck and J. Loris Martyn (Nashville: Abingdon, 1966), 217.

10. Martin Dibelius, *Studies in the Acts of the Apostles*, ed. Heinrich Greven (London: SCM Ltd., 1956), 155.

7

Homiletical Lessons from Paul

There is much that the student of preaching can learn from the Apostle to the Gentiles. He was a good model for personal Christian faith and conduct and for professional preaching performance. He demonstrated an art that can be studied and practiced. Paul claimed his past and his future for Christ. He did not discard the developed knowledge and skills that were acquired before his encounter with the Lord.

Handling Heritage

Christians can learn from Paul how to handle their past. A person can hide the past but he or she cannot hide *from* the past. Each individual is a product of his or her experience. We should learn from the past and use it in building the future. We should reflect on what we have learned formally and informally. What did you learn intentionally and what just happened? How did those who influenced you get your attention and make an impression? What would have made learning easier for you? What can you learn from your mistakes and your successes that will help you deal with others? The unexamined life is a bundle of wasted resources. That which we practice that is harmful to ourselves or others should be surrendered to the grace of God and that which can be utilized in Christian service should be turned over to Him for that purpose.

Personal Testimony

Paul had a personal experience with Christ which transformed his life. It was an experience which originally had to be interpreted for him (Acts 9:13-19; 22:1-13; 26:9-23; Gal. 2:11-15) but which became the source of life and ministry for him. Paul's preaching contained a strong confessional element. He bore witness to what he had seen, felt, and learned of Christ and to the effect that knowledge had on his life. Paul never hesitated to tell people how God had made Himself known to him and what God had done in his life (Mark 5:19). He shared with others his former misconceptions and how his mind had changed.

Every preacher should have an experience to share. It does not have to be dramatic or sudden, but it should point to the realization of Jesus as the revelation of God and as the agent of justification and reconciliation. Paul's preaching was powerful because he did not just know *about* God; he knew God. The knowledge which he had acquired about God as a Pharisee was given new meaning by the infusion of the Holy Spirit. Effective preaching has the character of witness.[1] It is the witness of the proclaimer and the witness of the community of faith.

Scholar-Preacher

Paul utilized all the knowledge and truth God had made available to him, that which came through the study of books, that which came from teachers, that which was observed in life, that which was intuitive, and that which came by way of special revelation. He never rejected knowledge in favor of ignorance nor did he demonstrate any fear of truth that came from non-Christian sources. God is the Creator and His imprint is on the natural order, including the human psyche. When a person is baptized, all of his or her skill should be baptized. The world of the Christian is not divided into sacred and secular. All should be sacred.

A Clear Call

Paul had a strong sense of divine call to his mission. He believed that he had been set apart to preach the gospel and commissioned to proclaim it to the Gentiles. Paul understood the Damascus road experience as a call (Gal 1:15; 1 Cor. 1:1) and he believed that others were called to preach (Rom. 10:14-15). Paul's call had all the characteristics of the classical prophetic call (Isa. 49:1*ff;* Jer. 1:4-10; Isa. 6:8-9). One must be careful not to confuse the nature of the call experience with the call, but one needs a sense of vocation to find the strength for the task. The work of preaching has in both Catholic and Protestant traditions been affirmed as a spiritual vocation. The call may be an impulse affirmed by the church or a sense of compulsion ignited in a dramatic experience. The consciousness of a call may come gradually or suddenly. It should have both intellectual and emotional content and should evoke a response of willing commitment. Preaching, Karl Barth wrote, is

> the attempt by someone called thereto in the church, in the form of some portion of the biblical witness to revelation, to express in his own words and to make intelligible to the men of his own generation the promise of the revelation, reconciliation and vocation of God as they are to be expected here and now.[2]

One would be hard put to find a better capsulization of the preaching of Paul or his theology of preaching for the church. The call was incentive, power, and witness for Paul and should be for all who preach.

Voice of the Community

Church as community of faith was important to the work of Paul. Ananias was instrumental in the call experience, Paul was nurtured among believers. Barnabas watched his growth and was used to call him to Antioch at the right time. The church at Antioch commissioned him and supported his work. Before the New Testament was canonized, Paul proclaimed the witness to the revelation of God. He expressed the revelation in words appropriate to each congregation, and he proclaimed the reconciling power of the gospel. The community of faith is usually instrumental in the call of an individual and should provide nurture for the development of gifts. Preaching is not a "Lone Ranger" activity; proclamation is the proclamation of the church. Antioch provided a material and spiritual base for Paul and each minister today needs a home base.

Paul believed that God worked through the preaching event to effect salvation. Paul had a very high view of the power of the proclaimed gospel. Preaching should never become routine or an empty ritual for preachers. Redemption is present in the words of preaching. The gospel includes claim and promise and evokes faith in those who will receive it. Again, the preacher should not think in terms of a solo performance. The preacher plays a role in an event which is best orchestrated by the Holy Spirit. If preachers do not have excitement and anticipation for preaching events, they cannot expect positive attitudes from congregations.

Good News for Whom?

Much of the excitement which attends accounts of Paul's preaching can be attributed to the missionary character of his ministry. Paul took on the difficult task of presenting the gospel to people who had not heard it before. He set out to tame hostile intellectual, moral, and spiritual environments as some love the challenge of taming undeveloped lands. He went to busy places where there were many people who had not heard the gospel. This does not mean he was engaged in mass evangelism for he often worked one on one or in the midst of a small group. He did, however, put his leaven in large loaves.

Paul worked in the epicenters of first-century society He penetrated population centers that promised a great harvest for carefully planted quality seed. He spoke in whispers or shouted as the occasion demanded. Like Jesus before him, he preached to one or many, by exposition of Scripture, interpretation of history, and analysis of the human condition. He went to where the people were and looked to the spread of the gospel.

The Preaching Art

The biblical record of Paul's preaching and the content of his epistles demonstrate the strong influence of classical Greek rhetoric. Paul's performance and analysis lends itself to categorization in the ancient canons of rhetoric, subject matter (invention), organization, style, mastery, and delivery. The principles of Paul's use of rhetoric may serve as standards or tools for the modern preacher. Preaching as defined by content and subject matter is the most important of the rubrics. Invention is an appropriate label for this aspect of communicating the gospel.

Personal and Professional

Paul invented the particular form of Christian rhetoric which we call Christian preaching. He had only the example of Jesus and the apostles. He synthesized the Greek and Jewish preaching traditions to create Christian preaching. Aristotle identified three modes of proof for use in the speaker's invention, *ethos, pathos,* and *logos. Ethos,* or character, Aristotle believed, "is the most potent of all the means to persuasion."[3] Being a preacher is more than a role. It is a state of being. Augustine observed that "the life of the speaker has greater weight . . . than any grandness of eloquence."[4] Paul preached out of his experience of living through the work of the Holy Spirit. He reported the continuing leadership of the Spirit in his work. He demonstrated the Christian life in his work and interpersonal relationships. Effective preachers will back up their words with a distinctive life-style.

Paul continued to work on personal spiritual development throughout his career. He wrote to the Philippians from a prison cell that he was not perfect and pressed "on toward the goal for the prize of the upward of God in Jesus Christ" (Phil. 3:15). He made prayer an important part of his testimony and teaching. Contemporary preachers must give a high priority to prayer. A life of prayer is essential to effective preaching. By "effective" I mean true to the gospel, not necessarily popular.

Knowledge, integrity, and goodwill are the personal qualities that Aristotle believed move listeners. The effective preacher must be broadly educated and trained to synthesize and utilize knowledge in the service of God. Augustine turned to the writings of Cicero to note that "eloquence without wisdom is often extremely injurious and profits no one."[5] Paul used every resource at his disposal to accomplish his purpose. He utilized literature, history, philosophy, and even the natural science of his day in the service of the cross. Paul drew on his Jewish and Greco-Roman education for communicating God's truth.

Integrity may suggest the proper use of knowledge as well as the spiritual wholeness of the preacher. Plato contended in his dialogues that the rhetorician must be a good person who knows the truth and how to divide it.[6] The preacher should be among the most diligent of scholars and the most educated of all people. The preacher must be trained in how to think and how to ask the right questions, that all of life may be a search for truth. Integrity emerges from the being of the preacher. Preaching cannot be separated from the character of the preacher. The preacher's credibility is rooted in what is perceived as personal spirituality. Paul not only had integrity but also made it known in such a way as to try to affect the perception of his character. Integrity must be visible but not in a self-serving, egotistical manner.

Messengers to All People

The preacher should be adept at cross-cultural communication that recognizes educational, cultural, economic, ethnical, and religious differences. *Pathos* may best be understood in terms of empathy. An audience will respond favorably to speakers who convince them that they share their struggles and feel *with* them. Paul was a master of this.

A pastor has a tremendous advantage over most speakers because of the extended and durable relationship which is possible with the audience. Preachers who want to know what they should preach, that is, what the people need to hear, should immerse themselves in the lives of the congregation. Paul did everything possible to do this. He lived with the people in order to identify with them. We cannot expect to communicate with people we do not understand. We must seek to learn value systems and how they were derived. Before we can speak in terms of "satisfying" needs, we must know those needs, as well as goals, successes, and failures.

Contact must be established on a human level on the "I-Thou" basis rather than the "I-it" basis upon which so many pastor-lay relationships rest. An I-Thou relationship requires a willingness on the part of preachers to expose themselves to the needs of others. The world with which Christ is concerned is the world of people. Directly and through all means available we must seek to include the world of labor, the world of the student, the world of the ghetto, the world of entertainment, the worlds of business, government, and sports. Too long we have insisted on playing on our own field, by our own rules and calendars. We have limited our witness to regularly organized church programs at assigned times. Instead of going into the world, we have dared the world to come to us. Paul invaded the daily lives of his congregations. He spoke boldly of their weaknesses as well as their strengths. He confessed his own sins and exposed his weaknesses to identify with and win their trust. Wendell Phillips observed that people are stimulated by an incarnated word.

> Truth never stirs up any trouble—mere speculative truth. Plato taught—nobody cared what he taught; Socrates acted, and they poisoned him. It is when a man throws himself against society that society is startled to persecute and to think.[7]

Involvement with people on the "gut" level will permit the pastor to see people in a new light and in turn to understand how their lives are determined. The typical congregation will respond to a sensitive preacher's grasp of the human situation and the divine response to it. Speakers may expect to be received only to the degree they have reduced anxieties and plugged into the dominant attitudes of the listeners.

The authority of preachers on a given occasion is directly proportionate to the degree of identification they achieve with the audience. Preachers must know what makes their listeners cry and what makes them laugh, what comforts them and what frightens them. Our sermons often supply salve where there is no pain. We scratch where there is no itch.

A Special Message

The relationship between speaker and listener is developed for the purpose of transmitting the *logos*. It is this third mode of proof that differentiates preaching from other forms of communication; the distinguishing factor is content, not method. Preaching is not preaching unless it is rooted in the Word of God. Preaching cannot be separated from interpretation of Scripture and theological construction. What is the revelation and how can it be translated into thought forms meaningful to contemporary audiences are fundamental issues for the preacher. Paul used Scripture as a primary source of authority but not with slavish literalism. Under the inspiration of the Holy Spirit, he reinterpreted Scripture in the light of the new revelation of Jesus Christ. Scripture was applied to his contemporary situation and that of his audience. Paul had a dynamic view of Scripture that made it a living word in the preaching event. Paul used typology to connect people and events of the past to later events, even current events. The preacher explains implications of the Scriptures.

Adequate treatment of *logos* requires not only knowledge of the subject, but also awareness of the structure of thought. How does the mind work? What convinces a person to want to change being and behavior? Speakers must not only have a clear purpose as to what they desire for the audience to believe or do but also a method to lead hearers to that conclusion or action. Paul's preaching demonstrates a careful analysis of each preaching context. He clarified issues and established theses as a basis for action. The preacher should identify the problem, truth, or fact, discover the cause, and establish the consequences of the situation. Even the use of common sense would strengthen much of what is passed off as preaching. Let the preacher be warned that arguments must be suited to the audience, for in a rhetorical situation proof always resides in the minds of the audience.

The recognition of the interrelation of reasoning, emotion, and personal appeal is essential to effective preaching. A sermon at its best is a particular message from a particular person on a particular occasion for a particular audience.

Structured Thought

The second canon of rhetoric is organization. The way an idea is presented can determine the success or failure of a sermon. Attention to such matters as establishing cause and effect, developing a logical climax, and presenting the most important points last can make a difference in audience response.

Ordering material in a coherent fashion will contribute to its retention. Writers such as Alan Monroe have suggested psychological patterns of organization modeled after John Dewey's system of reflective thinking. The idea is that the sequence should follow the course that might be expected in the thought process of personal problem solving. Dewey outlined the process as follows:

> Upon examination, each instance (of reflective thought) reveals, more or less clearly, five logically distinct steps: (1) a felt difficulty; (2) its location and definition; (3) suggestion of possible solution; (4) development by reasoning of the bearings of the suggestion; (5) further observation and experiment leading to its acceptance or rejection; that is, the conclusion of belief or disbelief.[8]

The most successful rhetorical act is one which *leads* the audience to arrive at the vision or decision you want to share. This may be accomplished indirectly leading them to journey where you have been. This pattern is a familiar one in a culture disposed to empirical method. Dewey related this method to scientific process.

> It places before others a map of the road that has been travelled; they may accordingly, if they will, retravel the road to inspect the landscape for themselves. The scientific investigator convinces others . . . by placing before them the specified course of experiences, searchings, doings, and findings in consequences of which certain things have been found.[9]

Paul often began in the past with his listeners, led them to the present, and then pointed in the direction of the future. As we observed in the study of his pattern, he often used the classical syllogism to lead them to what became an inevitable conclusion.

Living Language

Style is concerned with the material form, the symbolization of thought. Paul composed sermons for the ear and eye as well as the mind. He understood that the ear is for the preacher the gateway to the mind. His material is an excellent example of lively, picturesque language and vigorous rhythm. Language is symbolic action that requires careful selection of the words. Paul used, as should we, imaginative, emotionally charged language. His words could appeal to the senses and stir beautiful memories and inspiring visions of the future. The oral nature of preaching makes the choice and combination of words essential to effectiveness. The reader may pause and ponder; a difficult passage may be read again and again and every word analyzed. The listener, on the other hand, must hear aright the first time, and words must create vivid images which quickly form meaningful impressions in the mind. The speaker must choose precise, powerful diction in preference to the often abstract, denotative terms of the writers. Since the Middle Ages it has been popular to refer to language as the "dress of thought," but someone has suggested that it might be more appropriately termed "the incarnation of thoughts." Language, if it is to be effective, must have inherent energy. Vividness and impressiveness are desirable qualities. Language that grasps and holds on to the hearer, dramatic language that will "catch the conscience of the king," is the goal of the proclaimer. Paul did not shy away from strong, even provocative language when the occasion demanded it.

An Appropriate Medium

We know little about Paul's delivery. The clues that we have suggest that he was not a gifted orator in this regard. His critics believed him to be vulnerable at this point, "For they say, '. . . his bodily presence is weak, and his speech is of no account' " (2 Cor. 10:10). It is interesting to note that Paul responds to the charge in terms of comparison. Paul may not have been as eloquent as Apollos but he enjoyed too much success not to have had some competence in this area. Certainly some preachers are more naturally gifted than others, but his fact does not excuse those with lesser gifts from working to be the best they can possibly be.

Effective delivery is essential to communication. Those who fill the air with "sound and fury signifying nothing" are no more to be discredited than the boring passionless mumblers. The *Ad Herennium,* the earliest manual for the public speaker, identified the basic elements of good delivery. Vocal delivery requires conscious use of volume, stability, and flexibility. Physical movement "consists in a certain control of gesture and mien which renders what is delivered more plausible."[10] Hamlet's advice to the players is applicable for the pulpiteer:

> Speak the speech . . . trippingly on the tongue; but if you mouth it
> . . . I had as lief the town-crier spoke my lines. Nor do not saw
> the air too much with your hand, but use all gently. . . . Be not too
> tame neither, but let your own discretion be your tutor; suit the
> action to the word, the word to the action. . . .

Physical presence is an important factor in *ethos* as well as communication. The posture, muscle tone, facial expression, gestures, and movement of the preacher are as important as the language in transferring thought and more important in conveying feelings. Delivery and message are as inseparable in the moment of oral presentation as body and soul.

Delivery should be only a means to an end and is best when it is so integrated with the thought as to be indistinguishable from it. Rhetorical technique that draws attention to itself constitutes poor rhetoric. Delivery, however, is a kind of sieve through which thought is filtered. If it is clogged, nothing can pass through; it if is too open, impurities permeate the substance. The speaker should visualize the speaking art as involving the whole person. Thought, language, voice, and body must be coordinated. There should be consciousness of pitch, volume, and rate that will complement ideology. The necessary effort should be expended to develop clear articulation. Listeners should not be required to strain to hear but should be free to direct all their energy to apprehending intellectual content.

The final canon is one almost completely ignored today but of great importance in the first century—I refer to memory. Paul had to master and transport in his mind a great deal of material. It is unlikely that he ever read a speech in a public forum. He could speak on a moment's notice as an opportunity presented itself. The pastor is often given opportunity to express the Christian view at unexpected moments. The classical view of memory included a notion of information acquired, classified, and readily available. The preacher is expected to be a walking computer that can draw up biblical and theological knowledge at will. Moreover, clear images for translating that knowledge into relevant daily counsel are a tremendous asset.

A Special Aid

Paul taught that the greatest resource for the preparation and delivery of sermons is the Holy Spirit. He testified to the reliability of the Holy Spirit as guide and support for those called of God to proclaim His truth. The Spirit inspired the writers of Holy Scripture and likewise inspires those called to interpret Scripture. The Spirit will enlighten the mind of the preacher who allows time for prayer and meditation and who seeks the will of God. The Spirit preserves the tradition of the Church available in the great works of theology. The Spirit works in and through those who hear the preacher. There are times when the Spirit overcomes the poor words of a lazy preacher and accomplishes a divine purpose. The Holy Spirit will work at every stage of preparation and in the preaching event if the preacher is sensitive to His presence.

Notes

1. See John R. Claypool, *The Preaching Event* (San Francisco: Harper and Row, 1984), 85-110, and Thomas G. Long, *The Witness of Preaching* (Louisville: Westminster/John Knox, 1989).

2. Karl Barth, *Deliverance to the Captives* (New York: Harper and Row, 1961), 35.

3. *Rhetoric,* 9.

Homiletical Lessons from Paul

4. Ibid.

5. Augustine, *On Christian Doctrine,* trans. D. W. Robertson, Jr. (Indianapolis: Bobbs-Merrill, 1958), 121.

6. Plato, *Gorgias,* trans. W. E. Helmbold (Indianapolis: Bobbs-Merrill, 1952), and *Phaedras in The Works of Plato,* trans. Benjamin Jowett (New York: The Modern Library, 1928).

7. Wendell Phillips, *Speeches, Lectures, and Letters,* ed. Theodore C. Pease, Second Series (Boston, 1891), 396.

8. John Dewey, *How We Think* (Boston: D. C. Heath and Company, 1910), 72.

9. John Dewey, *Experience and Nature* (Chicago: Open Court Publishing Company, 1925), 11.

10. *Ad Herennium,* trans. Harry Caplan (Cambridge, Mass.: Harvard University Press, 1954), voice—191*ff.*; physical—201*ff.*

Bibliography

Achtemeier, Paul J. *Interpretation: A Journal of Bible and Theology (Paul the Apostle)*, vol. XLIII, no. 4. Richmond, Va.: Union Theological Seminary in Virginia, 1989.

Aristotle. *Rhetoric*. 1932; reprint. Trans. Lane Cooper. Englewood Cliffs, N.J.: Prentice-Hall, Inc. 1960.

Barth, Karl. *The Epistle to the Romans*. 1933 reprint. Trans. Edwyn C. Hoskyns. London: Oxford University Press, 1968.

Barth, Marcus. *Ephesians*. The Anchor Bible, vols. 34 and 34A. Garden City, N.Y.: Doubleday and Co., 1974.

Beaudean, John William, Jr. *Paul's Theology of Preaching*. Dissertation Series, no. 6. Macon: Mercer University Press, 1988.

Betz, Hans Dieter. *Galatians: A Commentary on Paul's Letter to the Churches in Galatia*. Hermenia. Philadelphia: Fortress Press, 1979.

Bornkamm, Gunther, *Paul*. Trans. D. M. G. Stalker. New York: Harper and Row. 1971.

Colson, Charles and Ellen Santilli Vaughn. *Against the Night: Living in the New Dark Ages*. Ann Arbor, MI: Servant Books, 1989.

Conzelmann, Hans. *I Corinthians: A Commentary on the First Epistle to the Corinthians*. Heremenia. Trans. James W. Leitch. Philadelphia: Fortress Press, 1975.

Dibelius, Martin. *Studies in the Acts of the Apostles*. Ed. Heinrich Greeven. 1956; rpt. London: SCM Press Ltd., 1973.

Dibelius, Martin and Werner Georg Kummel. *Paul*. 1953; reprint. Trans. Frank Clarke. Philadelphia: Westminister Press, 1966.

Bibliography

Dodd, C. H. *The Apostolic Preaching: Its Developments.* 1936; reprint. Grand Rapids: Baker Book House, 1980.

Dunn, James D. G. *Jesus, Paul, and the Law: Studies in Mark and Galatians.* Louisville: Westminster/John Knox Press, 1990.

Ellis, E. Earle. *Pauline Theology: Ministry and Society.* Grand Rapids: William B. Eerdmans Publishing Co., 1989.

Gartner, Bertil. *The Areopagus Speech and Natural Revelation.* Trans. Carolyn Hannay King. Acta Seminarii Neotestamentici Upsaliensis, vol. XXI. Uppsala: Almqvist and Wiksells, 1955.

Haenchen, Ernst. *The Acts of the Apostles: A Commentary.* Philadelphia: Westminister Press, 1971.

Hammerton-Kelly, Robert and Robin Scroggs. *Jews, Greeks and Christians: Religious Cultures in Late Antiquity.* Essays in honor of William David Davies. Leiden: E. J. Brill, 1976.

Harper, Nancy L. *Human Communication Theory: The History of a Paradigm.* Rochelle Park, N.J.: Hayden Book Co., Inc., 1979.

Hunter, Archibald M. *The Gospel According to St. Paul.* Philadelphia: Westminister Press, 1966.

Jones, J. Estill. *Acts: Working Together in Christ's Mission.* Nashville: Convention Press, 1974.

Kennedy, George A. *Classical Rhetoric and Its Christian and Secular Tradition from Ancient to Modern Times.* Chapel Hill: The University of North Carolina Press, 1980.

——————————. *New Testament Interpretation Through Rhetorical Criticism.* Chapel Hill: The University of North Carolina Press, 1984.

Kinneavy, James L. *Greek Rhetorical Origins of Christian Faith: An Inquiry.* Oxford: The Oxford University Press, 1987.

Mack, Burton L., ed. *Rhetoric and the New Testament.* Minneapolis: Fortress Press, 1990.

Malherbe, Abraham J. *Paul and the Popular Philosophers.* Minneapolis: Fortress Press, 1989.

Martin, Brice L. *Christ and the Law in Paul.* Supplements to Novum Testamentum, vol. LXII. Leiden: E. J. Brill, 1989.

Meeks, Wayne A. *The First Urban Churches: The Social World of the Apostle Paul.* New Haven: Yale University Press, 1983.

Morton, A. Q. and James McLeman. *Paul, the Man and the Myth: A Study in the Authorship of Greek Prose.* New York: Harper and Row, Publishers, 1966.

Murphy O'Conner, Jerome. *Paul on Preaching.* New York: Sheed and Ward, 1963.

Orr, William F. and James Arthur Walther. *I Corinthians.* The Anchor Bible, vol. 32. Garden City, N.Y: Doubleday and Co., 1977.

Patte, Daniel. *Preaching Paul.* Philadelphia: Fortress Press, 1984.

Richardson, Peter and John C. Hurd, eds. *From Jesus to Paul: Studies in Honour of Francis Wright Beare.* Ontario, Canada: Wilfrid Lavrier University Press, 1984.

Schweitzer, Albert. *The Mysticism of Paul the Apostle.* Trans. William Montgomery. New York: Henry Holt and Co., 1931.

Scott, C. A. Anderson. *Christianity According to St. Paul.* 1927; rpt. Cambridge: The Cambridge University Press, 1966.

Scroggs, Robin. *Paul for a New Day.* Philadelphia: Fortress Press, 1977.

Smith, David. *The Life and Letters of St. Paul.* New York: Harper and Brothers, Publishers, 1920.

Stendahl, Krister. *Paul Among Jews and Gentiles.* Philadelphia: Fortress Press, 1976.

Stewart, James S. *A Man in Christ: The Vital Elements of St. Paul's Religion.* New York: Harper and Brothers Publishers, 1935.

Stonehouse, N. B. *The Areopagus Address.* London: The Tyndale Press, 1949.

Wilder, Amos N. *Early Christian Rhetoric: The Language of the Gospel.* 1964; reprint. Cambridge, MA: Harvard University Press, 1978.

_____. *The New Voice: Religion, Literature, Hermeneutics.* New York: Herder and Herder, 1969.

Ward, Richard Finley. "Paul and the Politics of Performance at Corinth: A Study of 2 Corinthians 10-13." Ph.D. dissertation, Northwestern University, 1987.

Scripture Index

Paul the Preacher

Scripture Index

Paul the Preacher